ROUTLEDGE LIBRARY EDITIONS: LIBRARY AND INFORMATION SCIENCE

Volume 16

COLLECTION DEVELOPMENT IN SCI-TECH LIBRARIES

COLLECTION DEVELOPMENT IN SCI-TECH LIBRARIES

Edited by
ELLIS MOUNT

LONDON AND NEW YORK

First published in 1984 by The Haworth Press, Inc.

This edition first published in 2020
by Routledge
2 Park Square, Milton Park, Abingdon, Oxon OX14 4RN

and by Routledge
52 Vanderbilt Avenue, New York, NY 10017

Routledge is an imprint of the Taylor & Francis Group, an informa business

© 1984 The Haworth Press, Inc.

All rights reserved. No part of this book may be reprinted or reproduced or utilised in any form or by any electronic, mechanical, or other means, now known or hereafter invented, including photocopying and recording, or in any information storage or retrieval system, without permission in writing from the publishers.

Trademark notice: Product or corporate names may be trademarks or registered trademarks, and are used only for identification and explanation without intent to infringe.

British Library Cataloguing in Publication Data
A catalogue record for this book is available from the British Library

ISBN: 978-0-367-34616-4 (Set)
ISBN: 978-0-429-34352-0 (Set) (ebk)
ISBN: 978-0-367-36317-8 (Volume 16) (hbk)
ISBN: 978-0-367-36324-6 (Volume 16) (pbk)
ISBN: 978-0-429-34529-6 (Volume 16) (ebk)

Publisher's Note
The publisher has gone to great lengths to ensure the quality of this reprint but points out that some imperfections in the original copies may be apparent.

Disclaimer
The publisher has made every effort to trace copyright holders and would welcome correspondence from those they have been unable to trace.

Collection Development in Sci-Tech Libraries

Ellis Mount, Editor

The Haworth Press
New York

Collection Development in Sci-Tech Libraries has also been published as *Science & Technology Libraries,* Volume 4, Number 2, Winter 1983.

Copyright © 1984 by The Haworth Press, Inc. All rights reserved. Copies of articles in this publication may be reproduced noncommercially for the purpose of educational or scientific advancement. Otherwise, no part of this work may be reproduced or utilized in any form or by any means, electronic or mechanical, including photocopying, microfilm and recording, or by any information storage and retrieval system, without permission in writing from the publisher. Printed in the United States of America.

The Haworth Press, Inc., 28 East 22 Street, New York, NY 10010

Library of Congress Cataloging in Publication Data
Main entry under title:

Collection development in sci-tech libraries.

(The Science and technology libraries series)
 "Has also been published as Science & technology libraries, volume 4, number 2, winter 1983"--T.p. verso.
 Includes bibliographies.
 1. Technical libraries—Collection development—Addresses, essays, lectures. 2. Scientific libraries—Collection development—Addresses, essays, lectures. 3. Technology—Bibliography—Addresses, essays, lectures. 4. Science—Bibliography—Addresses, essays, lectures. I. Mount, Ellis. II. Series.
Z675.T3C58 1984   0.25.2'1865   83-22478
ISBN 0-86656-279-6

Collection Development in Sci-Tech Libraries

Science & Technology Libraries
Volume 4, Number 2

CONTENTS

Introduction	xi
The Development of Robotics and Its Literature: Overview with Bibliography *Janice F. Sieburth*	1
Background in Fiction and Fact	1
The Problem of Definition	3
Economic and Social Implications	4
The Emerging Literature of Robotics	5
Books on Robotics	8
Book Publishers	9
Bibliographies	9
Journals, Trade Periodicals, and Newsletters	10
Indexes and Abstracts	10
Databases	11
Conclusion	12
Bibliography	12
Acid Rain Information: Knee Deep and Rising *Robert E. Trumbule* *Marilyn Tedeschi*	27
Introduction	27
Bibliographies	30
Databases	32
Books and Monographs	33
Journals	34
Newsletters	35
Congressional and Other Legislative Branch Documents	35
Other Federal Agency Publications	37

Industry-Sponsored Research	38
State Activities	38
International Sources	38
Future Trends	39

Information Sources for Semiconductor Technology 43
Charles W. Moulton

Introduction	43
Primary Literature	44
Secondary Sources	48
Conclusions	53

Pest Management Literature: Collection Development 57
Syed M.A. Khan

Introduction	57
Place of Agriculture in the World Ecosystem	59
Pest Management Literature	59
Conclusion	86

A Guide to Information Sources in Genetic Engineering 89
Melinda E. Saffer

Introduction	89
Textbooks and Reference Sources	92
Laboratory Manuals and Methodology	93
Periodical Literature	94
Reviews of the Literature	96
Conference Proceedings	97
Patents	98
Regulations and Compliances	100
Abstracts and Indexes	100
Online Services	102
Conclusion	104

SPECIAL PAPER

Science and Technology Academic Facility Construction in Louisiana-Oklahoma-Texas, 1977–1982 109
Frank L. Turner
Bernard S. Schlessinger
Kristin Sandefur

Introduction	109
Methodology	111
Data from Questionnaires	112
Science-Technology Facilities	114

NEW REFERENCE WORKS IN SCIENCE AND TECHNOLOGY — 117
Robert G. Krupp, Editor

SCI-TECH ONLINE — 129
Ellen Nagle, Editor

Database News	129
Information Science Abstracts Available	131
Publications and Search Aids	132

SCI-TECH IN REVIEW — 135
Suzanne Fedunok, Editor

Publishing of Scientific Journals	135
A Model for Reference Service	136
Instruction in Chemical Literature	137
Robots in Libraries	138

Introduction

Building suitable collections for sci-tech libraries is a process of prime importance. Many users, when asked to evaluate sci-tech libraries, will list the strength of the collections high on the list of major criteria. Sci-tech collections are not the easiest ones to develop successfully in view of the complexity of the subjects involved, the large numbers of choices to make (because of the sizable quantity of books and journals from which to select), and the difficulty of even knowing about certain gray area publications, such as important but elusive proceedings of meetings, little known government documents, or obscure papers which appeared as technical reports.

In this issue five diverse subject areas are covered by writers who have a strong background of experience in dealing with their topics. In the first paper Janice F. Sieburth describes the growth of the field of robotics, a topic of great current interest, then lists important examples of pertinent books, serials and indexing services. The second paper, by Robert E. Trumbule and Marilyn Tedeschi, is devoted to acid rain, a topic of continuing concern, nationally and internationally. Besides traditional publications they emphasize major Federal documents worthy of note.

Semiconductor technology, which has acquired major importance because of its role in computers and other electronic devices, is dealt with in the paper by Charles W. Moulton, who includes major databases and current awareness literature along with monographic works. The fourth paper, by Syed M. A. Khan, discusses the literature on pest management, a subject of great significance to agriculturists and environmentalists. The last thematic paper, by Melinda Saffer, discusses the literature important in the field of genetic engineering, a major topic of interest.

The special paper for this issue is a survey of academic libraries dealing with sci-tech materials, recently built in the states of Louisiana-Oklahoma-Texas; it was prepared by Frank L. Turner, Bernard S. Schlessinger, and Kristin Sandefur.

Readers will note a new name among the section editors. Janice W. Bain has resigned as editor of *New Reference Works in Science*

© 1984 by The Haworth Press, Inc. All rights reserved.

and Technology, this due to the press of duties in her work at the Transportation Research Board. She did a commendable job as section editor. I am pleased to announce that her successor will be Robert G. Krupp, who was, until his recent retirement, Chief of the New York Public Library's Science & Technology Research Center. He brings a wealth of experience in sci-tech library matters to this position.

Ellis Mount, Editor

The Development of Robotics and Its Literature: Overview with Bibliography

Janice F. Sieburth

ABSTRACT. Present day industrial robots have resulted from technical advances in mechanical engineering, micro-electronics, and computers. The literature of the field reflects these varied components and is growing rapidly. While many developments have been evident in patents, technical reports and conference proceedings, the recent literature includes new books, journals, indexes and bibliographic databases. These publications are listed and sources of the literature on robotics are discussed. The changing nature of the field indicates the importance of current information and a growing interest in economic and social impacts of robotics.

BACKGROUND IN FICTION AND FACT

It was 1921 and robots were being manufactured by the thousands on a small island and shipped all over the world. The factory was R.U.R. (Rossum's Universal Robots) and the action took place in a play called *R.U.R.* by Karel Capek.[1] This play was responsible for establishing the word "robot" in the English language from the Czech word "robota" meaning forced labor. The mechanical men and women in the play eventually became the masters of the world. This image of an intelligent but sinister human counterpart was rein-

---

Janice F. Sieburth is Reference/Bibliographer for Physical and Engineering Sciences and Associate Professor at the University of Rhode Island Library, Kingston, RI 02881. She received BS and MS degrees from Washington State University and an MLS from the University of Rhode Island.

forced by Isaac Asimov's *I, robot*,[2] and other stories. However, one of Asimov's *Three laws of robotics* eventually set the code for robot conduct: above all they may not injure a human being. These negative portrayals have been followed by many others about generally more friendly robots or androids such as R2D2 and C3PO in the movie "Star Wars." Although worries about their personalities or motivations have diminished, intelligent machines still cause uneasiness and concern.

Actual robots have been complex and expensive machines until recently when less costly components became available. Robots or kits to build them have come on the market with names like HERO (Heath Co.), RB5X (RB Robot Corp.), GENUS (Robotics International), B.O.B. and TOPO (Androbot Inc.).[3] These are good instructional tools and are also inspiring the formation of hobbyist groups. There are predictions that just as there will soon be a personal computer in every home, next there will be a personal robot in every home.

Robots today are the result of the merging of significant technical advances in electrical and mechanical engineering and computer science. The beginning of true robotics is generally considered to be a patent in 1954 by George C. Devol, "the robot man,"[4] for a manipulator with a memory that controlled its sequential movements. This and subsequent patents became the basis for the world's largest robot producing company, Unimation, Inc. Joseph F. Engleberger, "Father of the robot,"[5] founded the firm and continues as president. He has done much to publicize and expand the use of robots and is the author of articles and a popular book: *Robotics in practice.*[6]

The first Unimate robot was sold to General Motors in 1961 and today the automobile industry utilizes about 60 percent of the nation's industrial robots. These robots have been used primarily for operations such as: hand/tool manipulations for welding, spray painting and drilling; parts handling—picking up pieces, moving them from place to place or inserting a piece in a hole; and assembly which involves joining up parts, inspection and finishing.

Although early developments took place in the United States, robotics did not make much of an impact on American industry for the next decade. Companies in Japan, however, were eager for advanced technologies and recognized the productivity potential of robot utilization. Japan acquired American patents in the early 1970s and soon achieved world leadership in the use and manufacture of robots. Japan's foremost position in the field is expected to continue for some time to come. Other countries such as Sweden, Germany and Italy, along with the United States, are now developing substantial inventories of industrial robots and at the end of 1981 there were estimates that Japan had 14,000 robots in use; the United States, 4,000; Soviet Union, less than 4,000; Sweden, 1,300; Germany, 1,200; Italy, 650 and 1,150 in the rest of Europe.[7] These numbers are expected to rise dramatically by 1995 when experts predict that the United States will have a population of 315,000 robots in industry.[8]

THE PROBLEM OF DEFINITION

Estimates of numbers of robots vary because there are different definitions for them. Simple automated machines have been counted by the Japanese, who feel that automation with flexible machines is robotic in nature. Other definitions of robots vary from simple "pick and place" mechanisms that move in a predetermined sequence to intelligent machines that imitate human activities, judgments and senses. To provide uniformity, the Robot Institute of America established this definition:[9]

> An industrial robot is a programmable, multifunctional device designed to manipulate and to transport material, parts, tools, or specialized manufacturing implements through variable programmed paths for the performance of specific manufacturing tasks.

Industrial robots must have certain essential components. (a) Manipulators: mechanical arms with joints that bend, twist, rotate, extend or elevate. Movement is described by degrees of freedom. (b) Hands: grippers or end-effectors that can hold and operate tools or lift and move objects usually by mechanical, vacuum or magnetic means. (c) A control mechanism (or brain): a microprocessor or computer which can be programmed for simple or complex sequential operations. Data can be stored for decision making and feedback. The controls may be directed by sensors such as machine vision, voice, touch or chemicals. (d) A power source: electrical, hydraulic or pneumatic. Higher level robots with distinct artificial intelligence have more degrees of freedom, are easier to teach or program, have larger memories, operate with precision and reliability, and are very versatile.

Standards have become important and ANSI (American National Standards Institute, Inc.) has initiated activities which will result in standards for the field of industrial automation.[10] This would include robotics, machine tools, control systems and materials handling and should lead to international standards in the field.

ECONOMIC AND SOCIAL IMPLICATIONS

Robots have advantages over a human labor counterpart. They don't tire or become bored with monotonous operations, they can fit parts with extremely small tolerance, they can work in toxic environments, they can work quickly and at a constant rate of speed and can carry very heavy loads. Declining costs of robots while human labor costs rise have made them particularly attractive to manufacturing industries. D'Ignazio[11] suggests that robots will become the slave class of modern society. They will work long hours taking care of the boring, hazardous and menial jobs and humans won't have to feel guilty about it.

Ayres and Miller in *Robotics applications and social implications*[12] discussed job loss and economic impacts caused by the introduction of robots in industrial processes while the "Upjohn report"[13] examined the potential impact of robots on the job market in Michigan. An article in the *IEEE Spectrum,* May 1983, asks about automation's effect on society and suggests that planning should be done to cope with potential problems.[14]

A study sponsored by the Society of Manufacturing Engineers and conducted by the University of Michigan was *Industrial robots: a Delphi forecast of markets and technology* which described the expanding robot markets.[15] The contributions of the robotics industry to "high tech" and the competitiveness of the U. S. industry in world markets was assessed in a 1983 conference sponsored by the Department of Commerce.[16] Participants deplored the lack of data availability, definition for a robot, an internationally accepted robot classification system and the competitive atmosphere which makes information difficult to obtain. Nevertheless, conclusions were that Japan would continue to dominate a market that will reach ten billion dollars by 1990 with the U. S. and western Europe each maintaining an equal share of the balance.

As developing technology improves the performance of industrial robots, their uses in other fields will be expanded. Suggested activities for robot populations are: exploring and mining under hazardous living conditions such as outer space and the deep sea, providing aid for disabled and handicapped people, working with hazardous chemicals including radioactive substances, firefighting, acting as household servants, police surveillance and defusing bombs. Areas of active research and development include software for easier and more complex programming, manipulators with improved flexibility, more reliable and sophisticated power transmission and communication systems and increased performance of sensing devices. As robots become more sophisticated and applications increase so will the quantity of technical literature and publications on economic and social impacts.

THE EMERGING LITERATURE OF ROBOTICS

The first literature on robotics was fiction. As functional robots became a reality, technical reports, patents and conference proceedings formed the embryonic literature of this developing field of technology. Utilizing information from the subject fields of the various components of the robots—mechanical engineering, industrial engineering, micro-electronics, and computers and control—the resulting composite literature reflects the growth pattern of the industry. As technical systems matured and applications increased, international meetings and symposia have been a major source for communication within the field. Published proceedings of these conferences are a significant portion of the literature. Journals, indexes, books and databases are now multiplying as the literature of robotics has evolved into a significant subject area.

Before the word robot became established as the term for intelligent mechanical devices, the word AUTOMATONS was used as an indexing term in the *Industrial arts index* published by the H. W. Wilson Co. between 1913 and 1957. The infrequent entries under this subject usually referred to articles on mechanical devices and gadgets which often used clock mechanisms. The earliest reference from this source on the term, robot, was for a brief note in *Scientific American* in 1929 answering a reader's query about the source of the word.[17] MACHINERY, AUTOMATIC indexed the more general subject area until the mid-1950s when AUTOMATION became firmly established in the index. When the *Applied Science and Technology Index* replaced the *Industrial Arts Index* in 1958, the term *AUTOMATION* yielded considerable entries. From 1960 on the term ROBOTS is consistently cross-referenced to AUTOMATONS until 1983 when ROBOTS and ROBOTS, INDUSTRIAL were established as direct subject headings.

In the *Engineering Index* articles on robots were included under INDUSTRIAL PLANTS—AUTOMATION through 1974 when INDUSTRIAL ROBOTS became an indexing term. In the 1983 issues, ROBOTICS has become a separate entry. These changes in subject headings indicate a certain maturity of the field and recognize the explosion of literature that is occurring in the 1980s.

Current primary sources of information are: industrial, government and laboratory reports; patents; conference proceedings; journal articles; society publications; and books. Older material and other relevant current literature can be found in the publications related to components of robots. These subject areas may include movements of mechanical joints, manipulators, computer control, micro-electronics, machine vision and computer-aided manufacture. The literature of industrial automation provides many examples of robot applications.

Technical reports are a source of much literature on robotics. The U. S. National Technical Information Service (NTIS) has recently recognized the importance of making available reports from both the United States and foreign countries with a recent expansion to include international sources. In late 1982, NTIS announced an agreement with the Japanese Ministry of Labor to secure their studies on the impact of micro-electronics based devices in the workplace. Some of the reports will be in English and NTIS will translate the most significant of the balance. New NTIS newsletters will provide current information on the latest technical reports.

The need for up-to-date information on developments in other countries has also encouraged the proliferation of conferences, particularly those with international participation. Exhibitions, which often accompany conferences, provide examples of the latest technology and the opportunity to see mechanical systems in operation. The first annual *National symposium on industrial robots* was held in 1970 while the first *International conference on industrial robot technology* took place in 1973. Some conferences held in the early 1980s include *Robots in the automotive industry, International conference on developments in mechanized, automated and robotic welding, International conference on robot vision* (3rd in 1983), *Advanced software in robots, Canadian CAD/CAM and robotics, Ap-*

plied machine vision conference, International conference on man/machine systems and the *National conference on artificial intelligence.*

Scientific organizations sponsor many of these conferences and international meetings will often be organized jointly by robotics societies from several countries. For instance the 10th *International symposium on industrial robots* was held jointly with the 5th *International conference on industrial robot technology* in Milan, Italy, in 1980. Sponsoring groups were: Italian Society for Industrial Robots, Italian Machine Tool Manufacturers' Association, *Industrial robot* journal, French Industrial Robot Association, British Robot Association, Institute of Production Automation, International Federation for Theory of Machines and Mechanisms, Japan Industrial Robot Association, Robot Institute of America and International Fluidics Services.

The Society of Manufacturing Engineers (SME) has been very active in the sponsorship of conferences as well as the publication of proceedings, technical papers and periodicals on robotics. A subgroup of SME, Robotics International, was formed in 1980 for the professional working in the field. Other organizations which have an interest in robotics and related topics and which contribute to the published literature include: American Management Association (AMA), American Society of Mechanical Engineers (ASME), Institute of Electrical and Electronics Engineers (IEEE), International Society for Optical Engineers (SPIE) and Society of Automotive Engineers (SAE).

Participants at conferences and authors of current reports and articles represent industry, government and academic environments. Funding for research programs comes from both the federal government and private industry. One of the largest and best funded academic programs is at Carnegie-Mellon. Other institutions which have active research groups include MIT, Stanford, Yale, George Washington University, and the Universities of Maryland, Minnesota and Rhode Island.[18]

Today, literature of robotics can be found in a wide range of scientific and technical sources. Technical reports, patents and conference proceedings form a core of robotics information that has mushroomed in the 1980s to encompass new books, new periodicals and new indexing sources. Professional societies offered strong bibliographic support to the growing field which is now supplemented by an increasing complement of trade publications. The general engineering literature will continue to provide additional information while publications in the social sciences will increase as robotics makes a greater impact on the labor force and our political and social systems.

BOOKS ON ROBOTICS

Books on the technology of robots, their applications and their future began to appear in the 1970s. Engelberger noted that a worldwide inventory of 71 robot firms was published in 1973 in *Industrie roboter* by Warnecke and Schrafft.[19] In 1979 Tanner edited a collection of articles and papers to produce a two-volume set on *Industrial robots: fundamentals and applications* and Allan's *A survey of industrial robots* reviewed the field in 1980. Second editions of these books were published in 1981 and 1982, respectively. Since 1980 the number of books on robotics has shown a sudden increase. Good surveys of the field are Engelberger's *Robotics in practice,* 1980, which describes robots in the manufacturing process, their management and uses; Albus, *Brains, behavior and robotics,* 1981, which discusses the relationship of the human brain and artificial intelligence, also covers applications of robotics; and D'Ignazio, *Working robots,* 1982, which provides a less technical overview of the field. An understanding of the Japanese view of the robotics industry, their applications and future predictions is offered by the Japan Industrial Robot Association, published by Prentice-Hall, in *The robotics industry of Japan today and tomorrow,* 1982. This view of the competition lists at $525 for 581 pages.

Reference books which encompass the field of robotics are few, but announcements of forthcoming books indicate that this gap in the literature will soon be filled. The *Robotics Industry Directory* is now published yearly. *Robotics Today* has announced an annual edition in hard cover. The 1982 volume includes the contents of the previous ten issues of the periodical, a manufacturer's directory and a bibliography of SME papers published between 1974 and 1979. *The Industrial Robot* has produced a special issue to commemorate ten years of publication. Besides short articles by prominent figures in the field (that cover some of the history of robots, design, applications, management and future potential), there is an alphabetical listing of about 250 of the world's robot manufacturers and suppliers that includes their agents in other countries.

BOOK PUBLISHERS

Major technical book publishers such as Elsevier/North Holland, McGraw-Hill, Pergamon, Plenum, Prentice-Hall and Wiley are currently listing at least one scholarly book on some aspect of robotics. Other publishers who are committed to relevant book series include the MIT Press with its *Series in artificial intelligence* which lists *Robot manipulators,* 1981, and *Robot motion,* 1982. Springer-Verlag published the first two volumes of their *Scientific fundamentals of robotics series* in 1982. IFS (Publications) Ltd. has announced a new series, *International trends in manufacturing technology* with *Robot vision* the first title. IFS publishes other books along with magazines, marketing reports and conference proceedings on robotics and advanced automation in industry.

Professional societies such as the American Society of Mechanical Engineers (ASME), American Management Associations (AMACOM) and the Society of Manufacturing Engineers (SME) also publish books on robotics. The SME has a lengthy list of titles in the series, *Manufacturing update series,* which covers new trends in industrial processes. Two editions of *Industrial robots* are included in this series. One of SME's newest books is *Industrial robots: a Delphi forecast of markets and technology,* which illustrates their interest in both the marketing and technical aspects of the field.

Smaller, more specialized publishers which are producing books on robotics include the Digital Press; Industrial Press, Inc.; Leading Edge Publishing, Inc. and Robotics Press. TAB Publishers supply the how-to books for hobbyists and the classroom with titles such as *How to build your own self-programming robot* and *Robot intelligence...with experiments.*

BIBLIOGRAPHIES

Several bibliographies are now available on robotics. The Society of Manufacturing Engineers (SME) has produced a listing of the articles, conference proceedings and papers which the Society has published between 1974 and 1982. Gomersall and Farmer in their 1981, *Robotics bibliography,* cover a broader scope of sources and include more than 2,000 references published between 1970 and 1981.

United States patents on industrial robots have been collected in a technical report from NTIS. Copies of the front page and first page of specifications have been included for 212 patents of which half originated in other countries including Japan, West Germany, Sweden, France as well as others. This collection illustrates the technical advances and where they originated. NTIS also publishes a search of the NTIS data base going back to 1965. The latest update on robots to March 1982 includes 243 reports. Topics covered are design, software development, control problems, mechanical studies and uses.

For an historical look at the contributions made by the Massachusetts Institute of Technology (MIT) on artificial intelligence which includes basic robotics, Comtex Scientific Corp. is making available a complete collection on microfiche of over 500 memoranda representing work done between 1958 and 1979. There is an accompanying index and online access to this collection which is available through the Bibliographic Retrieval Services.

JOURNALS, TRADE PERIODICALS, AND NEWSLETTERS

The first English language journal on robotics was *The Industrial Robot* which began just a decade ago in 1973. Emphasis on industry and international concerns has continued with articles on the latest developments, case studies, market reports and planning studies. Periodicals in related fields which have indicated an editorial interest in robotics in more recent years include: *Computers and Industrial Engineering, Mechanisms and Machine Theory* and *Production Engineering*. New journals and newsletters have multiplied in the 1980s, many of them emphasize reports on new developments in technology, new applications and hardware, software and market news. Trade journals which include advertisements provide another source of information on equipment and suppliers. Some of the newest titles are: *International Journal of Robotics Research* from the MIT Press, *Robotica: International Journal of Robotics* published by Cambridge University Press, and *Automation News,* "First newspaper of the robotics industry."

INDEXES AND ABSTRACTS

Two new indexing journals have begun publication since 1982. *Robotics Technology Abstracts* from the Cranfield Press, England, provides monthly abstracts of journal articles, technical reports, patents and conference proceedings. The *Robomatix Reporter* from

EIC/Intelligence was scheduled to begin in April 1983. Monthly abstracts would have broad subject coverage with emphasis on the robotics industry and marketing concerns. Advertising for this index describes it as an "integrated information system" and indicates that it will also be available as a database through the major vendors.

Engineering and science indexes are sources for the literature of robotics technology and its various aspects. Indexing may be under ROBOTS or ROBOTICS, INDUSTRIAL ROBOTS, AUTOMATONS or AUTOMATA. Related terms are: ARTIFICIAL INTELLIGENCE, AUTOMATION, COMPUTER-AIDED MANUFACTURE, COMPUTER APPLICATIONS, KINEMATICS, MACHINE VISION, MANIPULATING DEVICES, PATTERN RECOGNITION, SENSORS or SERVOMECHANISMS. *Business Periodicals Index* offers access to non-technical industry, market and business publications for information on the economic impacts of robotics as well as applications and utilization in the industrial setting.

Sources of current awareness are very important for such a rapidly changing and competitive field. *Current Contents: Engineering Technology and Applied Sciences* and *Key Abstracts: Systems Theory* provide weekly and monthly access to the literature, respectively, as soon as possible after publication. NTIS has just begun weekly abstracting newsletters: *Manufacturing Technology* and *Foreign Technology* which will publish summaries of new reports from the United States and other countries on high technology topics. *The Industrial Robot* also includes a section of abstracts of current international publications in the quarterly issues.

DATABASES

Bibliographic databases which contain a significant number of citations on robots and robotics are listed in the bibliography along with the major vendors which supply them. Vendors included are the Bibliographic Retrieval Services (BRS), Latham, NY; Dialog Information Services, Palo Alto, CA; and the System Development Corporation (SDC), Santa Monica, CA.

Free-text searching by truncating the word stem robot may yield irrelevant citations when source documents are international in scope. Polish and Czech document titles may be retrieved where the meaning is work or labor not related to the English meaning of robots. For the purpose of this paper, databases were scanned for citations using robot, robots or robotics and those with more than 500 hits have been included. Highest postings in scientific and technical databases were for INSPEC, a file of over 2,000,000 records derived from *Physics Abstracts, Electrical and Electronics Abstracts* and *Computers and Control Abstracts;* COMPENDEX, from the *Engineering Index;* and ISMEC, a mechanical engineering database. WELDASEARCH, CONFERENCE PAPERS INDEX, SCISEARCH and NTIS were good sources of citations. The CONFERENCE PAPERS INDEX from 1973 on, with a total of over 944,000 records, had a slightly higher retrieval than EI ENGINEERING MEETINGS, which only began in 1979 and contains about 66,000 records. Both databases will retrieve individual papers from published proceedings of conferences.

Among the business databases Predicast's F & S INDEXES and PROMT were both excellent sources of citations and the TRADE AND INDUSTRY INDEX also supplied a substantial list of references. MAGAZINE INDEX is a good source for articles from popular magazines.

CONCLUSION

Robots have been on the covers of many popular magazines in early 1983 and articles on robot applications, conferences, market projections and announcements of new technical developments appear regularly in science and engineering journals. Active well-funded research programs, industrial demands for new technologies to improve productivity and less costly, more versatile robots will help maintain the momentum of this technical field. Current information and literature on the various component parts of robots as well as the increasingly diversified applications will become even more important.

BIBLIOGRAPHY

Books—Reference

Allan, J. J. *A survey of industrial robots.* 2nd ed. Dallas, TX: Leading Edge Publishing, Inc.; 1982.

Overview of robotics field, practical aspects of incorporating robots into an operation and comparison of robots from 48 manufacturers with capabilities, significant features, purchase and installation information.

Decade of robotics: Special tenth anniversary issue of the Industrial Robot Magazine. Bedford, England: IFS (Publications) Ltd.; 1983.
   Short articles reviewing history, current uses of robots, design, management and future. Listing of world's robot manufacturers.

Hunt, V. Daniel. *Industrial robotics handbook.* New York: Industrial Press, Inc. Announced for 1983.
   Overview of industrial robots: hardware, types, functions and future.

Robotics Industry Directory. La Canada, CA: Robotics Publications Corp.; 1982- . Annual.
   Includes names and addresses of robot distributors, consultants, sources for components and peripherals, research laboratories, robot manfacturers in Japan. Details of robots, specifications, contact personnel included.

Robotics Today Annual Edition. Dearborn, MI: Society of Manufacturing Engineers; 1982- . Annual.
   Hard cover edition for 1982 includes ten issues of *Robotics Today,* Summer 1979 to Fall 1981; subject, issue indexes; manufacturers directory; titles and abstracts of SME papers on robotics from 1974 to 1979.

Safford, Edward L. *Handbook of advanced robotics.* Blue Ridge Summit, PA: TAB Books; 1982.
   History of robots, types, mechanics, installation and general overview of design and applications.

Tver, David F.; Bolz, Roger. *Robotics sourcebook and dictionary.* New York: Industrial Press, Inc. Announced for 1983.
   Includes terminology, applications of robots, lists of companies with products and relevant computer terms.

Books—General

Albus, James S. *Brains, behavior and robotics.* Peterborough, NH: Byte/McGraw-Hill; 1981.
   Computers simulate processes in the brain producing artificial in-

telligence, and mechanisms of machines are compared with those of humans. Implications for future generations of robots are considered along with economic and social effects.

Ayres, Robert U.; Miller, Steven M. *Robotics, applications and social implications.* Cambridge, MA: Ballinger; 1983.
 General overview of robotics technology with discussion of impact on labor force, social and political systems.

D'Ignazio, Fred. *Working robots.* New York: Elsevier/Nelson Books; 1982.
 Overview of robots and varied uses from undersea prospecting to household servants. Discusses role in the classroom and basics for building your own.

Engelberger, Joseph F. *Robotics in practice: management and applications of industrial robots.* New York: AMACOM; 1980.
 Analysis of industrial robots, their components, advantages in the manufacturing process, applications and the future.

Industrial robots. Vol. 1. *Fundamentals.* Vol. 2. *Applications.* 2nd ed. Tanner, William R., ed. Dearborn, MI: Society of Manufacturing Engineers; 1981.
 Reprints of articles and papers provides the basics of robotics including implementation, utilization, capabilities and applications in the first volume. Second volume is primarily case studies of uses of robots from die casting to loading boxes.

Japan Industrial Robot Association. *The robotics industry of Japan today and tomorrow.* Englewood Cliffs, NJ: Prentice-Hall; 1982.
 Analysis of Japan's use of robots in both manufacturing and non-manufacturing applications. Includes labor costs and other economics, current trends and future projection.

Book Series

International trends in manufacturing technology. Bedford, England: IFS (Publications) Ltd.
 Robot vision. Ed. by Pugh, A., 1982.
 Projected: *Robot welding.*
  Programmable assembly.

Manufacturing update series. Dearborn, MI: Society of Manufacturing Engineers.
   Selected titles:
      Industrial robots, 1979.
      Manufacturing cost estimating, 1980.
      Achieving success in manufacturing management, 1980.
      Industrial robots, 2nd ed., 1981.

MIT Press series in artificial intelligence. Cambridge, MA: MIT Press.
   Selected titles:
      Artificial intelligence, an MIT perspective, 1979.
      Ullman, Shimm. *The interpretation of visual motion,* 1979.
      Grimson, William; Leifur, Eric. *From images to surfaces; a computational study of the human early visual system,* 1981.
      Paul, Richard P. *Robot manipulators: mathematics, programming, and control: the computer control of robot manipulators,* 1981.
      Robot motion: planning and control, 1982.

Scientific fundamentals of robotics. New York: Springer-Verlag.
   Vukobratović, Miomir. *Dynamics of manipulation robots: theory and application,* 1982.
   Vukobratović, Miomir. *Control of manipulation robots: theory and application,* 1982.

Bibliographies

Artificial intelligence memoranda of the AI Laboratory, Massachusetts Institute of Technology (1958-1979). New York: Comtex Scientific Corp.; 1983.
   Over 513 complete documents on microfiche. Author, title indexes.

Bibliography of SME robotics materials. Dearborn, MI: Society of Manufacturing Engineers; 1982.
   References with abstracts of articles from *Manufacturing Engineering* and *Robotics Today,* conference and technical papers published by and available from the Society of Manufacturing Engineers. Includes 342 citations from 1974-1982.

Gomersall, Alan; Farmer, Penny. *Robotics bibliography, 1970-1981.* Bedford, England: IFS (Publications) Ltd.; 1981.

Includes over 2,000 citations covering robot design and performance, development of sub-systems and peripherals, sensors, control theory and systems, robot applications and patents.

Industrial robots: a survey of foreign and domestic U. S. patents. Springfield, VA: U. S. National Technical Information Service; 1982; PB 82-169269.

Covers 212 U. S. patents on industrial robots issued between 1969 and March 1982. Full copies of the patents are on microfiche in back pocket.

Robots: citations from the NTIS data base, 1964-March, 1982. Springfield, VA: U. S. National Technical Information Service; 1982 May; PB 82-808395.

Bibliography with abstracts of 243 reports primarily on design and applications of robots.

Journals, Trade Periodicals, and Newsletters

Automation News. New York: Grant Publications; March 1983- Monthly (may become a weekly by 1984).

"First newspaper of the robotics industry." Intended to feature automation and robotics events, hardware and software news, market and financial reports, commentary.

Computers and Industrial Engineering: an International Journal. New York: Pergamon; vol. 1- , 1977- . Quarterly.

Areas of interest include robotics, physical simulation, computer-aided manufacture.

The Industrial Robot. Bedford, England: IFS (Publications) Ltd.; vol. 1- ; 1973- . Quarterly.

International coverage of industrial robotics including specifications, coming events, new products and books and abstracts of current articles.

Industrial Robots International. Ft. Lee, NJ: Technical Insights; vol. 1- ; 1980- . Semi-monthly.

Emphasis on use of robots in manufacturing. Information on technical meetings, new equipment, technology, patents, reports, applications.

International Journal of Robotics Research. Cambridge, MA: MIT Press; vol. 1– ; 1982– . Quarterly.
  Broad coverage of robotics science including electrical and mechanical engineering, computers and software, artificial intelligence, automatic control.

The Japan Robot News. Tokyo: Survey Japan; vol. 1– ; 1982– . Quarterly.
  Emphasis on the robotics industry and the use of industrial robots.

Mechanisms and Machine Theory. New York: Pergamon Press; vol. 7– ; 1972– . Bi-monthly.
  Official publication of the International Federation for the Theory of Machines and Mechanisms. Subject areas include man-machine systems and robots, mechanical systems, dynamics of machines. (Preceded by *Journal of Mechanisms,* vol. 1-6, 1966-1971.)

Production Engineering. Cleveland, OH: Penton/IPC, Inc.; vol. 24– ;1977– . Monthly.
  Sponsored by the Institution of Production Engineers, American Institute of Industrial Engineers and the Society of Manufacturing Engineers. "The productivity publication." Emphasis on current developments. (Preceded by *Automation,* vol. 1–23, 1954–1976.)

Robot News International. Bedford, England: IFS (Publications), Ltd.; 1981– . Monthly.
  Newsletter with emphasis on current news and forthcoming developments. Covers people, new companies, robot applications, research, control systems, management and labor news.

Robot Systems and Products. La Canada, CA: Robotics Publications Corp.; 1982– . Monthly.
  New products, systems, applications, specifications. Updates the annual *Robotics Industry Directory.*

Robotica: International Journal of Robotics. New York: Cambridge University Press; vol. 1– ; 1983– . Quarterly.
  "International journal of information, education and research in robotics and artificial intelligence."

Robotics Age. Peterborough, NH: Robotics Publications Corp. 1981– . Bi-monthly.
Technical articles related to design and implementation of intelligent machines.

The Robotics Report. Annandale, VA: Washington National News Reports, Inc.; vol. 1– ; 1981– .
"Authoritative Washington report on the robotics industry."

Robotics Today. Dearborn, MI: Society of Manufacturing Engineers; 1979– . Bi-monthly.
Emphasis on new developments in industrial robot technology with emphasis on applications in manufacturing operations.

Robotics Update. Boca Raton, FL: Robotics Newsletter Associates; vol. 1– ; 1983– . Monthly.
Emphasis on new developments, products, applications and software systems. *Annual Buyer's Guide to Robotics* is also produced.

Sensor Review. Bedford, England: IFS (Publications) Ltd.; vol. 1– ; 1981– . Quarterly.
Emphasis on sensor technology in advanced manufacturing processes. Includes developments in inspection, measurement, robotics production, machine monitoring.

Frequent articles relating to robotics:

Artificial Intelligence.
Assembly Automation.
Control Engineering.
FMS Magazine.
High Technology.
IEEE Transactions on Automatic Control.
IEEE Transactions on Systems, Man and Cybernetics.
Industrial Engineering.
Machinery and Production Engineering.
Mechanical Engineering.
Production.
Production Engineering.
Production Research.

Indexes and Abstracts

ROBOTICS:

Robomatix Reporter. New York: EIC/Intelligence; April, 1983- . Monthly, annual index.

Coverage includes international science, technical and business journals, conference proceedings, government reports, laboratory research studies, university monographs, corporate reports and market forecasts. About 100-150 summaries per issue. Each issue has a monthly article on a current topic of interest with emphasis on current developments. Indexes: subject, author, source, industry (SIC), and corporations.

Robotics Technology Abstracts. Bedford, England: Cranfield Press; vol. 1- ;1982- . Monthly.

Worldwide coverage of journals, technical reports, patents and conference proceedings. Emphasis on manufacture and applications of robots. First issues include about 100 abstracts each.

ENGINEERING:

Applied Mechanics Reviews. New York: American Society of Mechanical Engineers; vol. 1- ; 1948- . Monthly, annual index.

World-wide sources include journals, books, conference, reports. Covers robot manipulators, automatic control, kinematics, assembly applications, sensing. Author, subject indexes.

Applied Science and Technology Index. New York: H. W. Wilson Co.; 1913- . Monthly, quarterly and annual cumulations.

Subject index to over 200 English language periodicals in technical fields which include computer technology and applications, electrical, industrial and mechanical engineering.

Electrical and Electronics Abstracts. London: Institution of Electrical Engineers; vol. 1- ; 1898- . Monthly, semi-annual indexes.

Sources include international journals, books, reports, dissertations and conference papers. Electronics emphasis including instrumentation, sensing systems, pattern recognition, electrical machines. Indexes: subject, author, corporate author, conference, book, bibliography.

Electronics and Communications Abstracts Journal. Riverdale, MD: Cambridge Scientific Abstracts, Inc.; vol. 1- ; 1967- . 10 issues/year, annual index.

Coverage of journals, government reports, conference proceedings, books, dissertations, patents. Subjects include electronic systems and applications, sensors, artificial intelligence, computer-aided manufacturing and electronic devices. Subject, author indexes.

Engineering Index. New York: Engineering Information, Inc.; vol. 1- ; 1884- . Monthly, annual cumulation.

Abstracts international technical literature with broad coverage of journal articles, reports, monographs, conferences. Includes industrial applications, components, design and computer-aided-manufacturing. Subject, author, author affiliation indexes.

Index to Scientific and Technical Proceedings. Philadelphia, PA: Institute for Scientific Information; 1978- . Monthly, annual cumulation.

Indexes selected published proceedings, both the meetings and the individual papers. Approximately 35% are from engineering, technology and applied sciences. Indexes: Subject, author and editor, sponsor, meeting location, categories, corporate geographic index, corporate organization.

International Aerospace Abstracts. New York: American Institute of Aeronautics and Astronautics; vol. 1- ; 1961- . Semi-monthly; quarterly, semi-annual, annual indexes.

International coverage of journals, books, conference proceedings and papers, translations of journals and journal articles. Complements *Scientific and Technical Aerospace Reports.* Subject areas include man/machine technology, cybernetics, mechanical engineering. Source for outer space research utilizing robotics. Indexes: author, subject, report number, accession number.

Science Citation Index. Philadelphia, PA: Institute for Scientific Information; 1964- . Bi-monthly, annual cumulation.

Broad coverage of over 3600 primary journals in engineering and sciences, symposia, monographic series, multi-authored books and patents. *Source, Permuterm* and *Citation* sections. Author, corporate author, cited author and subject indexes.

COMPUTERS AND CONTROL:

Computer and Control Abstracts. London: Institution of Electrical Engineers; vol. 1- ; 1966- . Monthly, semi-annual indexes.

International sources include journals, books, reports, dissertations and conference papers. Computer aspects of robotics, artificial intelligence, man-machine and control systems. Indexes: Subject, author, corporate author, conference, book and bibliography.

Computer and Information Systems Abstracts Journal. Riverdale, MD: Cambridge Scientific Abstracts; vol. 1- ; 1962- . Semi-monthly, annual index.

Abstracts worldwide journal articles, government reports, conference proceedings, books, dissertations and patents. Subjects include computer aspects of robotics, artificial intelligence, manipulating devices, sensors, pattern recognition and computer-aided manufacture. Acronym, subject, author, and source indexes.

Technical Reports

Government Reports Announcements and Index. Springfield, VA: U. S. National Technical Information Service; vol. 1- ; 1946- . Semi-monthly, annual index.

Index to U. S. government sponsored research, development and engineering reports and translations. Subjects include robot development, servomechanisms, control systems, computer applications, manipulators. Foreign reports on new technologies are being added. Indexes: Subject, author, corporate author contract/grant number, NTIS order/report number.

Scientific and Technical Aerospace Reports. Washington, D. C.: U. S. National Aeronautics and Space Administration; vol. 1- ; 1963- . Semi-monthly, annual index.

Covers scientific and technical reports on man/system technology, with emphasis on aeronautics and space research. Indexes: Subject, author, corporate author, contract number, report/accession number.

Non-Technical Index

Business Periodicals Index. New York: H. W. Wilson Co.; 1958- . Monthly, quarterly and annual cumulations.

Subject index to English language business periodicals. Emphasis on economic and industrial aspects. Includes robotics industry, competition, computer technology and applications.

Current Awareness

Current Contents: Engineering, Technology and Applied Sciences. Philadelphia, PA: Institute for Scientific Information, vol. 1- ; 1970- . Weekly.
   Provides tables of contents of current journals. Subjects include mechanics, instrumentation/control and electronics. Author, brief subject indexes.

Foreign Technology Abstract Newsletter. Springfield, VA: U. S. National Technical Information Service; 1983- . Weekly.
   Abstracts of the latest scientific and technical reports from other countries including Japan, United Kingdom, France, and USSR. Annual subject index.

The Industrial Robot. Bedford, England: IFS (Publications) Ltd.; vol. 1- ; 1973- . Quarterly.
   Each issue contains an abstracts section with 40 to 50 entries of current international literature that includes journal articles, reports, and conference papers.

Key Abstracts: Systems Theory. London: Institution of Electrical Engineers; 1978- . Monthly.
   Topics covered include man-machine systems, cybernetics, pattern recognition, artificial intelligence selected from the "more important journals and conference proceedings." Not more than 250 items per issue.

Manufacturing Technology Abstract Newsletter. Springfield, VA: U. S. National Technical Information Service; 1983- . Weekly.
   New developments in government-sponsored research in robotics and CAD/CAM. Annual subject index.

Databases

ARTIFICIAL INTELLIGENCE AND ROBOTICS DATABASE. New York: Comtex Scientific Corp.; 1958 to 1979.
   Provides access to the artificial intelligence collection of Massa-

chusetts Institute of Technology. Expected to be updated with Stanford's artificial intelligence collection and other regular updates. Available from BRS.

COMPENDEX. New York: Engineering Information, Inc.; 1970- .
Over a million records, monthly updates.
Corresponds to *Engineering Index*. Available from BRS, Dialog and SDC.

CONFERENCE PAPERS INDEX. Bethesda, MD: Cambridge Scientific Abstracts; 1973- . Over 944,000 records, monthly updates.
Provides references to papers from over 1,000 regional, national and international scientific and technical meetings per year. Available from Dialog.

EI ENGINEERING MEETINGS. New York: Engineering Information, Inc.; 1979- . Over 66,000 records, updated monthly.
Indexes significant published proceedings of engineering and technical conferences, symposia, meetings and colloquia. Available from Dialog and SDC.

EIC/ROBOTICS. New York: EIC/Intelligence; 1983- .
Corresponds to the same printed title. Announced as an online database to be made available from the major vendors.

INSPEC. London, England: Institution of Electrical Engineers; 1969- . Over two million records, updated monthly.
Corresponds to *Physics Abstracts, Electrical and Electronics Abstracts* and *Computer and Control Abstracts*. Available from BRS, Dialog and SDC.

ISMEC. Bethesda, MD: Cambridge Scientific Abstracts; 1973- . Over 140,000 records, updated monthly.
Information service in mechanical engineering. Available from Dialog.

MAGAZINE INDEX. Menlo Park, CA: Information Access Corp.; 1976- . Over 689,000 records, updated monthly.
Source of articles in general magazines, broad subject coverage. Available from Dialog.

NTIS. Springfield, VA: National Technical Information Service; 1964- . Over 957,000 records, updated biweekly.
Corresponds to *U. S. Government Reports Announcements and Index.* Available from BRS, Dialog and SDC.

PREDICASTS F & S INDEXES. Cleveland, OH: Predicasts, Inc.; 1972- . Over 2,000,000 records, weekly updates.
Contains international company, product and industry information. Available from BRS and Dialog.

PREDICASTS PROMT. Cleveland, OH: Predicasts, Inc.; 1972- . Nearly 600,000 records, weekly updates.
Provides overview of markets and technology from international newspapers, magazines and reports. Available from BRS and Dialog.

SCISEARCH. Philadelphia, PA: Institute for Scientific Information; 1970- . Over 4,500,000 records, updated semi-monthly.
Corresponds to *Science Citation Index.* Covers general science and engineering. Available from Dialog.

TRADE AND INDUSTRY INDEX. Menlo Park, CA: Information Access Corp; 1981- . Over 322,000 records, monthly updates.
Index to trade and industry journals, business newspapers and other industry publications. Available from Dialog.

WELDASEARCH. Cambridge, England: The Welding Institute; 1967- . Over 64,000 records, monthly updates.
Covers all aspects of joining of metals and plastics and other welding and metallurgy topics. Available from Dialog.

Professional Societies

International Institute for Robotics (IIR). Dallas, TX
Promotes interest and research in robotics. Founded in 1960. Publishes *Robotics Newsletter.*

Robot Institute of America (RIA). Dearborn, MI.
Promotes the use of robotics technology in the United States and works with international organizations. Founded in 1974. For users, manufacturers, equipment suppliers, research institutes and educa-

tional institutions. Publishes *Robotics Today*. Presents the Joseph F. Engelberger medal annually to three outstanding individuals who have contributed to the science and practice of robotics.

Robotics International of SME (RI/SME). Dearborn, MI.
For robotics professionals. Affiliated with the Society of Manufacturing Engineers. Founded in 1980. Provides continuing education and certifies professionals in the field of robotics.

REFERENCES

1. Capek, Karel. *R. U. R.* In: Tucker, Samuel Marion, *Twenty-five modern plays*. New York: Harper and Brothers; 1931: p. 751-783.
2. Asimov, Isaac. *I, robot*. New York: Grosset; 1950.
3. Ruby, Daniel J. Computerized personal robots. *Popular Science*. p. 98-100; 1983 May.
4. Ayres, Robert; Miller, Steve. Industrial robots on the line. *Technology Review*. 85(4):35-47; 1982 May/June.
5. Bell, John. We'll have robots like ladies have hats. *New Scientist*. 97(1346): 528-529; 1983 February 24.
6. Engelberger, Joseph F. *Robotics in practice: management and applications of industrial robots*. New York: AMACOM; 1980.
7. Poised for explosive growth. *Standard and Poor's Industry Surveys*. 2:M26-M28; 1983 January.
8. Hegland, Donald E. No end in sight. *Production Engineering*. 30(4):47-51; 1983 April.
9. Dratch, Ralph L. Plugging into robotics. *Consulting Engineer*. 60(4):60-65; 1983 April.
10. Stauffer, Robert N. Industrial hazards to impact robots. *Robotics Today*. 5(2):71; 1983 April.
11. D'Ignazio, Fred. *Working robots*. New York: Elsevier/Nelson Books; 1982.
12. Ayres, Robert; Miller, Steven. *Robotics applications and social implications*. Cambridge, MA: Ballinger; 1983.
13. Hunt, H. Allan; Hunt, Timothy L. *Human resource implications of robotics*, as reported in: Schreiber, Rita R. New perspectives: the Upjohn report. *Robotics Today*. 5(2):61-62; 1983 April.
14. Guterl, Fred. An unanswered question: automation's effect on society. *IEEE Spectrum*. 20(5):89-92; 1983 May.
15. *Industrial robots: a Delphi forecast of markets and technology*. Dearborn, MI: Society of Manufacturing Engineers; 1982.
16. *High technology industries; profiles and outlooks. The robotics industry*. Washington, D. C.: U.S. Department of Commerce; 1983 April.
17. Just what is a robot? *Scientific American*. 141:64; 1929 July.
18. Amram, Fred M. Robotics: the human touch. *Robotics Today*. 4(2):28; 1982 April.
19. Warnecke, Hans-Jurgen; Schraft, R. D. *Industrie-roboter*. Mainz: Krausskopf; 1973, as mentioned in: Engelberger, Joseph F. *Robotics in practice: management and applications of industrial robots*. New York: AMACOM; 1980: p. xvi.

Acid Rain Information: Knee Deep and Rising

Robert E. Trumbule
Marilyn Tedeschi

ABSTRACT. This article briefly describes the dramatic growth in acid rain literature which has occurred in the past five years and examines various sources of that information. Included among these are: bibliographies, databases, journals, newsletters, books and monographs, congressional and Federal agency documents, industry-sponsored research, State activities, and international sources. The article implicitly suggests that, while the sources one would use depend to a great extent on the purpose for which the information is sought, a careful selection of one bibliography, a few journals and newsletters, and a careful perusal of both congressional and executive agency documents should provide a good overview to where the best sources of knowledge on specific facets of the acid rain issue can be found.

INTRODUCTION

Acid rain is a term which, until about 10 years ago, was known only to a few scientists in rather specialized fields of ecology and environmental science. Now, however, it is practically a household word, is the subject of serious discussion between the United States and Canada, and is being hotly debated in the United States Congress.[1]

Robert E. Trumbule, a Specialist in Environmental and Energy Policy, is employed in the Environment and Natural Resources Policy Division of the Congressional Research Service, a part of the Library of Congress. He is a chemical engineer from the University of Pennsylvania, and has analyzed the acid rain issue for Congress since 1974.

Marilyn Tedeschi is an Information Resources Assistant on assignment with the Environment and Natural Resources Policy Division of the Congressional Research Service. Her responsibilities include the maintenance and expansion of the division's library and providing reference assistance to its analysts.

This paper represents the views of the authors and not necessarily those of the Congressional Research Service of the Library of Congress.

© 1984 by The Haworth Press, Inc. All rights reserved.

Simply put, acid rain is precipitation in any form which is more acidic than normal. It is widespread, occurring over most of eastern North America, central Europe and Scandinavia, as well as other parts of the world. Its causes are believed to be, for the most part, manmade air pollution (in particular oxides of both sulfur and nitrogen), with electricity-generating utilities burning fossil fuels bearing much of the blame. Other contributors include smelters, mobile sources (cars and trucks), and other industrial activities such as oil refining.

Typically, the rain falling in eastern North America is 10 to 100 times more acidic than normal. Acidity of this degree is believed to be responsible for the "death" of nearly 200 lakes in the Adirondack Mountains in New York and several thousand in Canada. It is also suspected of causing damage to forests in certain susceptible areas. For example, red spruce trees in some pristine areas of New England show reduced growth rates and there are only about one half as many living today as were living in 1965. West Germany now believes that 7.7 percent of their forest area has been damaged. Much of this is believed to stem from changes in soil chemistry associated with acid rain.

Acid rain also is believed to cause damage to buildings and other manmade structures. One estimate places damage to structures in the eastern third of the United States from acid rain at $2 billion per year in 1978 dollars.

Human health effects have not been proved; however, concern is expressed in two areas: (1) heavy metals (lead, mercury, cadmium, aluminum, etc.) that are mobilized by changes in the acidity of the soil may find their way into drinking water supplies; and (2) aerosols (fog, smog) of extremely high acidity may cause respiratory problems and may, in some way, be linked to observed high occurrences of lung cancer.[2]

Regardless of whether or not all the current fears of acid rain's effects prove true, the concern has led to a dramatic increase in the literature surrounding the subject. In fact, it has reached flood proportions. What was a trickle of articles in the early phases of research into this subject has now reached almost unmanageable proportions, especially if one has the task of maintaining at least a cursory knowledge of progress in all facets of acid rain research. Examination of a bibliography developed by EPA's Corvallis Laboratory[3] reveals that the average number of acid rain related articles from 1911 to 1950 was only about 1 to 2 per year but that this increased to about 11 per year from 1964 to 1968, 50 per year during 1969 to 1972, and 110 per year in 1973 to 1977. In 1978, there were 240 articles and in 1979, 324. As of January 1980, this particular bibliography contained approximately 1800 entries. Corvallis researchers have told us that the database now contains over 4000 items and will contain nearly 10,000 by 1984.

Both the growth rate of information on acid rain and the absolute number of articles available are not surprising. The dramatic growth in the database reflects both the seriousness with which the issue is viewed and the intensity of the policy debate occurring within our legislative bodies, both at the Federal and State levels. The large number of articles results primarily because the acid rain issue has so many facets: sources, transport, atmospheric chemistry, effects (lakes, streams, soils, forests, crops, man-made structures), economics, control technology, and international relations, to name but a few. Thus, sometimes it appears that there is almost no subject that cannot be given an acid rain twist. (There is even a fairly substantial number of acid rain cartoons in the principal author's file at the Library of Congress.)

The large number of items in the database also stems from a congressional belief that generally speaking, more science at this time will permit better policy decisions. This desire for obtaining more scientific information is reflected in the Federal budget. Federal funding for acid rain research in the late 1970s was generally around $10 million although this number is imprecise since the research was scattered throughout many agencies and not necessarily categorized as "acid rain" research. Then in 1980, Congress passed the Acid Precipitation Act as Title VII of the Energy Security Act, Public Law 96-294. This Act established a comprehensive 10-year research program to identify the causes and effects of acid precipitation and established a Federal Acid Precipitation Task Force to coordinate the research being conducted by or through twelve Federal agencies, administrations, or authorities and four national laboratories. Funding was established at $5 million per year for each of the fiscal years 1981 through 1990. This funding is in addition to what already existed. Thus, total funding for Federal acid rain research was $18.3 million for FY 1982, $22.3 million for FY 1983 and is proposed to be $27.6 million in FY 1984. One can readily see that the literature has yet to reflect the results of most of this funding and that soon the number of new articles on acid rain entering the database should become even more dramatic.

The purpose of this short article is to guide the relative newcomer to acid rain research along useful pathways through this swamp of literature.

BIBLIOGRAPHIES

Bibliographies are a logical place to begin to search when looking for policy analysis and technical information on acid rain. Federal and State agencies, the private sector and environmental organizations are examples of the diversified types of institutions and entities conducting and publishing research on acid precipitation. In addition, foreign countries such as Sweden and Canada have in print a wealth of documents on the subject.

Some examples of these bibliographies are: *An Acid Rain Bibliography* (EPA), *Health and Environmental Effects of Acid Rain* (National Library of Medicine), *Reference Bibliography on "Acid Rain"* (Bituminous Coal Research, Inc.), *Acid Precipitation in Minnesota* (Minnesota Pollution Control Agency) and *Acid Rain* (Commonwealth Agricultural Bureaux, England). Detailed descriptions of these follow:

EPA's *An Acid Rain Bibliography* is a comprehensive collection of over 4000 titles of documents from 1911 to 1981 concerning acid rain. Collected in the bibliography are materials from scientific and environmental journals, conference proceedings, technical reports, and Federal and State government research projects and publications. There is also a large representation of European and Canadian material.

Topics covered include long range transport and transportation; deposition; natural and acid ecosystems; effects on materials, soils, sediments; natural sulfur and nitrogen cycles; and material on legal, economic, social and health effects.[4]

While widespread public awareness of the acid rain issues is a comparatively recent phenomenon, this bibliography first appeared in 1980 and has been revised on four occasions since its initial appearance. The most recent edition was published in 1981 to include newly published material and earlier citations brought to the editor's attention since the previous edition. The documents, reports and articles for the bibliography were compiled by Danny L. Rambo, of Northrop Services, Inc. under contract to EPA's Corvallis Laboratory. Mr. Rambo identified publications to be included in the bibliography from a number of sources, including collections on deposit at EPA, that agency's own research, principal actors in the field and other bibliographies, and book reviews in subject related journals.[5]

The bibliography is available on microfiche in two forms: an alphabetical list of titles with citations/abstracts and an author index. It also can be obtained in hard copy in two versions: a double volume of 1110 pages, which includes abstracts, and a shorter, 563 page version without abstracts. The entire bibliography is stored in a data base which is described elsewhere in this article.

Health and Environmental Effects of Acid Rain is a bibliography prepared in cooperation with the National Library of Medicine for the Information Response to Chemical Crises Project. An objective of the Project is to share information on topics of common interest to the members of the Project—acid rain is such a subject.

The topics covered include the environmental and health effects of acid precipitation and also the atmospheric chemistry that leads to its formation.

A research directory is included at the end of the bibliography, complete with information about current research projects. There is an index arranged by citations of the subject categories. Also included is a permuted title index with a numerical reference for each title.

The private sector, especially the coal burning industries, are publishing information. *Reference Bibliography on "Acid" Rain* was done by Bituminous Coal Research, Inc., an independent organization conducting research for the coal industry. Their acid rain research is sponsored by the National Coal Association. Completed in July 1980 and expected to be updated within the next year, this bibliography contains 555 references of technical information on acid precipitation. The bibliography is alphabetically arranged by author and, in the case of a corporate author, article title. Each reference is sequentially numbered for each of the citations, as documents are cited by number in a General Subject Index which appears at the end of the volume. The citations are referenced under twelve subject categories: Analyses, Conferences, Deposition, Effects of Acid Rain, Long-Range Transport, Modelling and Models, Monitoring Networks, Oxidation, pH Measurement, Reviews, Sources, Washout. Listed below each index term are the numbered references that are categorized under that term.

Most of the publications listed are available from Bituminous Coal Research, Inc. However, additional sources for the documents accompany each citation. This appears to be adequate to facilitate acquisition of materials of interest.

Acid Precipitation in Minnesota includes research projects conducted in Minnesota and vicinity, and general and technical articles. They are listed alphabetically by author and chapter.

The Commonwealth Agricultural Bureaux (CAB) of England provides an information service for researchers in the agricultural community. Scanning over 8,000 journals for articles of agricultural interest, the CAB regularly reproduces abstracts of specialized topics into bibliographies—*Acid Rain* is one such topic.[6]

The bibliography is divided into two parts: (1) General—which contains abstracts on occurrence of acid rain and conferences concerning acid rain; and (2) the effects of acid rain on the ecosystem. The abstracts are detailed, and the number of references each cited article includes is given.

DATABASES

Listed below are the main databases and files to use when looking for information on acid rain.

1. *Library of Congress Computerized Card Catalog (LCCC).* This database, maintained by the Library of Congress, lists books catalogued at the Library since 1968. New acquisitions to the Library's collection are added every two weeks, making this database a good source to find new monographs published about acid rain.

2. *Lockheed DIALOG System.* There are nine files in this system which are the best to use for acid rain searches:

To search for technical information:

> APTIC— Contains resources on all areas of air pollution, including abstracts of selected literature from the holdings of the Air Pollution Technical Information Center.
> ENVIROLINE—Contains on-line abstracts from the Environment Information Center, Inc.'s publication *Environment Abstracts.*
> ENVIRONMENTAL BIBLIOGRAPHY—Periodicals pertaining to water, air, soil and health hazards are cited in this file.
> POLLUTION ABSTRACTS—Abstracts technical related literature to pollution sources and control. This database corresponds to the publication *Pollution Abstracts.*

To search for general information:

MAGAZINE INDEX—370 popular American magazines are indexed in this file.

NEW YORK TIMES INFOBANK—Covers current affairs and contains citations with detailed abstracts to 15 daily newspapers and 43 journals.

To search for Government publications:

NTIS—Government-sponsored research reports and journals are cited.

To search for international publications:

PAIS INTERNATIONAL—The database of the Public Information Service, containing international publications that are social science orientated. The journals, books and Federal and State documents and reports cited are listed in English, French, Italian, Portuguese, and German.

3. *RECON.* RECON contains the energy-related databases produced or obtained by the Department of Energy's Technical Information Center. Acid rain information can be found in the ENERGY DATA BASE.

As mentioned before, *An Acid Rain Bibliography* is a product of the database kept by EPA's Corvallis Laboratory. The files are publicly accessible by using a qualified operator of FAMULUS, a free form storage and search software package.[7]

Currently, the information from Corvallis Laboratory is being merged with the RECON/ENERGY DATA BASE. This will result in an expanded database that covers not only the environmental effects of acid rain, but also the energy-related effects.

BOOKS AND MONOGRAPHS

The Library of Congress' computerized card catalog contains 41 references to books or monographs dealing with acid rain. If one subtracts references to congressional hearings documents, 28 citations remain. These include conference proceedings and short monographs, the latter presenting, for the most part, strongly pro-control environmentalist views or anti-control, industry views. If both conference proceedings and monographs are excluded, the remaining books are mostly general overviews of the acid rain issue and probably do not represent the most efficient avenue of access to insight. The books are sometimes longer than necessary, and superficial in their treatment of the issue. A much more effective aproach is to select a few overview journal articles on the subject.

One exception to this generally negative view of currently available books written on acid rain is one by Wetstone and Rosencranz of the Environmental Law Institute.[8] Entitled "Acid Rain in Europe and North America," it provides an excellent summary of existing law and proposed legislative solutions relating to acid rain both in Europe and North America, and, in the process, provides a very good overview of the subject.

JOURNALS

As the environmental and scientific communities were the first to develop sensitivity to the acid rain problems, it is the journals of these communities that were the print forum of first report for published research and policy analysis on the subject. In these journals one can find articles of widely varying complexity, ranging from general overview pieces to detailed scientific analyses. Examples of these magazines are: *Environmental Science and Technology, Journal of the Air Pollution Control Association, Nature, Ambio, Chemical and Engineering News,* and *Combustion.*

No longer a closed topic of the environmental and scientific community, articles on acid precipitation can now be found in the popular press. Glance at the magazine rack as you check out of the grocery store. *Newsweek* has a cover story on acid rain, while *Boston Magazine* writes about "The Quiet Death of the Quabbin," a reservoir that provides Boston's water supply.

But although these articles are included in journals that EPA's bibliography considers "gray literature,"[9] they are often an excellent means to educate the average person on why acid rain should concern them.

Robert H. Boyle's article, "An American Tragedy," written for *Sports Illustrated,* is an excellent example. The article describes the effects of acid rain on lakes and wildlife. At first glance this article might seem to be keeping strange company with the latest professional draft picks and four-minute milers. However, lakes are major sites for a number of popular aquatic sports such as swimming, boating, water skiing, and fishing, as well as popular vacation centers for the general public. Any compromise to the environment which would diminish the attraction for these sports is of interest and concern to the user public.

NEWSLETTERS

Newsletters, usually daily to bi-weekly in frequency, and about four to 12 pages in length, often contain a concise and current view on acid rain. These are extremely useful for keeping abreast of developments in Federal policy affecting acid rain. The newsletters generally report on private and public sector research, describe legislative activity with the U.S. Congress and congressional interaction with the executive branch, and provide insight into organizational developments within the agencies that affect the policy-making process. *Energy Daily, Inside EPA, Inside Energy/Federal Lands,* and National Wildlife Federation's *Conservation 83* are examples.

A new and important member of this group is *Acid Precipitation Digest.* Published bi-monthly by the Center for Environmental Information, Inc., located in Rochester, New York, the *Digest* is devoted exclusively to all aspects of acid rain. Included in the *Digest* are short news capsules, a calendar of events, and a list of recent meetings. Current literature is reviewed and new articles given mention. Information on how to obtain copies of all printed material and whom to contact for information on meetings is included for all items mentioned in the *Digest.*

CONGRESSIONAL AND OTHER LEGISLATIVE BRANCH DOCUMENTS

Congress has given, and continues to give, thorough oversight of the acid rain issue. Early congressional awareness was shown by the House Science and Technology Committee's Subcommittee on the Environment and the Atmosphere then chaired by George Brown (D. Calif.).[10] Since then, there have been more than 15 congressional publications, mostly in the form of congressional hearings records, dealing with acid rain either directly or indirectly. While most of these documents will have the term "acid rain" in their titles, many deal primarily with other issues such as the Clean Air Act, conversion of power plants to coal, or environmental effects of increased fossil-fuel combustion, so the careful researcher must be certain to cast his net broadly enough to capture these documents. In fact, if one regularly reviews the activities and scans the publications of just a few congressional committees, most documents relating to acid rain will be found. These key committees include: (1) Senate Committee on Energy and Natural Resources; (2) Senate Committee on Environment and Public Works; (3) Senate Committee on Foreign Relations; (4) House Committee on Energy and Commerce; (5) House Committee on Government Operations; (6) House Committee on Interstate and Foreign Commerce; and (7) House Committee on Science and Technology.

Congressional documents are of particular value to researchers seeking broad understanding of the state of research in the field of acid rain, the state of development of technology to control it and the policy implications of any potential legislative actions.

Most witnesses appearing before Congress are carefully chosen to provide broad perspectives of both sides to controversial issues and those testifying on acid rain matters are no exception. Congressional testimony to date contains the full spectrum of information and opinion from all sides—industrialists, environmentalists, scientists and engineers. Most often they represent the best in their field and consequently they provide, both in their testimony and in documents submitted for the record, the ultimate in what is known about the subject. Therefore, the careful researcher would be well advised to use this source early on, if not first, in his effort to gain a broad understanding of the issue. A partial list of congressional hearing documents appears in Appendix I.

Congress has several research arms providing information and analyses. These include: (1) the Congressional Budget Office (CBO); (2) the Congressional Research Service (CRS); (3) the Government Accounting Office (GAO); and (4) the Office of Technology Assessment (OTA). Each of these congressional organizations has staff very knowledgeable about the acid rain issue who have been advising Congress on the matter for several years. While these organizations produce documents which are primarily for Congress and its staff, from time to time major studies are released for wider distribution.[11] Often the reports of their analyses appear in various daily or weekly newsletters (*Inside EPA* or *Energy Daily*, for example), or in larger databases. Once a researcher has ascertained that a congressional support agency document exists, it can usually be obtained by contacting either the publication office or the public information office of that agency or the Government Printing Office. Failing that, contact with your congressional representative may be considered.

OTHER FEDERAL AGENCY PUBLICATIONS

Similar advice can be given for documents published by other Federal agencies. The executive branch is conducting or funding the bulk of the acid rain research. The Interagency Task Force on Acid Precipitation, headed by three agencies—the Department of Agriculture, the National Oceanic and Atmospheric Administration, and the Environmental Protection Agency—and composed of 9 other executive department agencies and authorities, has the responsibility for coordinating all federally sponsored and conducted acid rain research. The Task Force's *Annual Report, 1982* (published June 8, 1983) summarizes the state of the science, and the research progress to date and provides an outlook for future efforts.

The Environmental Protection Agency has a very large role in the acid rain research effort as revealed by its $14 million FY 1983 acid rain budget. The agency has published a draft of "The Acidic Deposition Phenomenon and Its Effects: Critical Assessment Review Papers." The Friday, May 20, 1983, issue of the *Federal Register* provided official notice that this draft document was available for public review and comment for a 90-day period.

Other Federal agencies have published significant acid rain work. Those most likely to do so are on the previously mentioned Federal Acid Precipitation Task Force. They are the Departments of Agriculture, Commerce, Energy, Health and Human Services, Interior, and State; the Environmental Protection Agency; the National Oceanic and Atmospheric Administration; the National Aeronautics and Space Administration; the Council on Environmental Quality; the National Science Foundation; the Tennessee Valley Authority; and the four national laboratories—Argonne, Brookhaven, Oak Ridge and Pacific Northwest.

To mention all or even a sampling of work by each of these organizations is beyond the scope of this article. Most of their work will ultimately be reported in one of the larger databases discussed elsewhere in this article.

INDUSTRY-SPONSORED RESEARCH

One of the most significant industry-sponsored, acid-rain-related programs is being conducted by the Electric Power Research Institute (EPRI). This article would be incomplete without reference to the excellent summary provided by EPRI of their research into the issue.[12]

This 73-page document summarizes the $16.4 million in research conducted by EPRI through 1982 and outlines their proposed 1983-1987 $67.7 million efforts. Research areas discussed include: atmospheric chemistry, deposition, aquatic processes, crop production, forest production, economic evaluations and decision tools.

STATE ACTIVITIES

Many States are developing databases related to acid rain problems and research within their own boundaries. This is especially true of the North Central, Central and North Eastern States. The best way to access this information is to contact the appropriate office within each State. This is most readily accomplished by consulting the *1983 Conservation Directory*[13] published by the National Wildlife Federation. It provides addresses and phone numbers of all State departments of natural resources and is a quick way to find the knowledgeable persons on acid rain within each State.

INTERNATIONAL SOURCES

Several countries other than the U.S. have contributed significantly to understanding acid rain. Sweden, West Germany and Canada have done particularly important work.

Much of the original concern about acid rain came from Sweden. While most of their work has been reported in the literature and is captured by databases reported elsewhere in this article, much work is still being done. The Swedish effort seems particularly strong on the study of mitigation attempts (liming of acidified lakes and streams).[14]

West Germany has conducted significant acid rain research especially on soil chemistry and forest effects.

Canada, of course, has had a major effort going in acid rain research, especially that pertaining to long range transport. Much of their research has been reported through the Canada/United States Research Consultation Group and the Canada/United States Work Groups, the latter established in 1980 under the Memorandum of Intent (to ultimately achieve a joint resolution of the transboundary air pollution problem). These work groups have done much work, have drafted a report and are proceeding with separate United States and Canadian peer reviews of their product. This report probably will be published in the fall of 1983.

Contact with the embassies of Sweden, West Germany, and Canada can lead to useful information regarding the research programs within each country. For information on the joint Canada/U.S. effort, either the Embassy of Canada in Washington, D.C., or the U.S. Department of State can help.

The Organization for Economic Cooperation and Development (OECD) with headquarters in Paris, France, has done work on transboundary air pollution and acid rain problems in Europe and may prove to be a useful source.

Similarly, the Council of the European Communities (EEC), located in Brussels, Belgium, may be of assistance. It is examining the problem of European transboundary air pollution and is attempting to develop policies which, if passed, would be binding on member countries.

FUTURE TRENDS

The introduction of new articles dealing with acid rain into the existing databases will accelerate as newly funded research is reported. However, database growth similar to that which occurred between approximately 1979 to present is not expected. That growth was primarily due to a retrospective review of the literature in which articles from many disciplines were found to pertain to acid rain even though they were not originally labeled (or even thought of) as acid rain research. Now that the retrospective review is largely complete, the growth in the acid-rain labeled literature will continue, but at a more reasonable pace. Nevertheless, the job of staying "on top" of the issue will continue to be a difficult one. All of us will need all the help we can get. We hope that this article has provided a bit of assistance.

REFERENCES

1. An excellent historical perspective of the acid rain issue is available. See: Cowling, Ellis B. Acid precipitation in historical perspective. *Environmental Science and Technology.* 16(a): 110A-123 A; 1982 February.
2. Winchester, John. Lung cancer in Florida may be linked to acid air pollution. *Air Quality Communique, American Lung Association of Florida.* 1(1):1-3: 1983.
3. Rambo, Danny L. *An acid rain bibliography.* Corvallis, Oregon: U.S. EPA Corvallis Environmental Research Laboratory; 1980 August; CERL-053. 68 p.
4. Rambo, Danny L. *The EPA Acid Rain Bibliography—what it is, what's available.* Corvallis, OR: U.S. EPA Environmental Research Laboratory; 1980 Aug. 1 p. (Information sheet).
5. Personal communication with Mr. Danny Rambo.
6. Ridout, L. M. *Acid rain.* Farnham Royal, Slough, England: Commonwealth Agricultural Bureaux; 1982 August; Annotated Bibliography No. F25. 62 p.
7. Rambo, Danny L. *An acid rain bibliography.* Corvallis, OR; U.S. EPA, Corvallis Environmental Research Laboratory; 1980 August; CERT-0-53. 68 p.
8. Wetstone, Gregory; Rosencranz, Armin. *Acid rain in Europe and North America.* Washington, D.C.: Environmental Law Institute; 1983.
9. Rambo, Danny L. *The EPA Acid Rain Bibliography—what it is, what's available.* op cit.
10. U.S. Congress. House. Committee on Science and Technology. Subcommittee on the Environment and the Atmosphere. *Research and development relating to sulfates in the atmosphere.* Committee Print, 94th Congress, 1st session. Washington: U.S. Govt. Print. Off.; 1975 June. Prepared for the Committee by the Environmental Policy Division, Congressional Research Service, Library of Congress.
11. An excellent example of work done for Congress by its research support agencies is OTA's "Regional Implications of Transported Air Pollutants: An Assessment of Acidic Deposition and Ozone." The interim draft of this document was published in July 1982, with the final draft expected in the summer of 1983.
12. Allan, Mary Ann; Perhac, Ralph M. *Acid precipitation research at EPRI.* Palo Alto, CA: Electric Power Research Institute; 1983 March.
13. National Wildlife Federation. *1983 conservation directory.* [May be ordered at $9.00 per copy + $1.55 shipping charge from N.W.F., 1412 16th Street. N.W., Washington, D.C. 20036].
14. An excellent overview of the Swedish view of the acid rain problem is found in: *Acidification today and tomorrow* published by the Swedish Ministry of Agriculture in 1982.

APPENDIX I

CONGRESSIONAL DOCUMENTS RELATING TO ACID RAIN

U.S. Congress. House. Committee on Energy and Commerce. Subcommittee on Health and the Environment. *Acid precipitation (Parts 1 and 2).* Hearings, 97th Congress, 1st session. Oct. 1, 2, 6, and 20, 1981. Washington; U.S. Govt. Print. Off.; 1982.

U.S. Congress. House. Committee on Government Operations. Environment, Energy, and Natural Resources Subcommittee. *Clean Air Act and increased coal use: Environmental Protection Agency oversight.* Hearings, 96th Congress, 1st session. Sept. 11 and 13, 1979. Washington: U.S. Govt. Print. Off.; 1979. 326 p. LRS79-17046.

U.S. Congress. House. Committee on Interstate and Foreign Commerce. Subcommittee on Health and the Environment. *Clean Air Act oversight—1980.* Hearings, 96th Congress, 2d session. June 16, 1980. Washington: U.S. Govt. Print. Off.; 1980. 218 p. "Serial no. 96-151" LRS80-9616.

———*Oversight—Clean Air Act amendments of 1977.* Hearings, 96th Congress, 1st session, on oversight hearings to examine how the Clean Air Act is working to control air pollution throughout the country. Washington: U.S. Govt. Print. Off.; 1980. 856 p. Hearings held July 30-Nov. 28, 1979. "Serial no. 96-110" LRS80-3033.

U.S. Congress. House. Committee on Interstate and Foreign Commerce. Subcommittee on Oversight and Investigations. *Acid rain.* Hearings, 96th Congress, 2d session. Feb. 26 and 27, 1980. Washington: U.S. Govt. Print. Off.; 1980. 784 p. "Serial no. 96-150" LRS80-9257.

———*Clean Air Act amendments of 1977—oversight.* Hearing, 96th Congress, 1st session. Apr. 9, 1979. Washington: U.S. Govt. Print. Off.; 1980. 52 p. "Serial no. 96-136" LRS80-6193.

U.S. Congress. House. Committee on Science and Technology. Subcommittee on Natural Resources and Environment. *Acid rain.* Hearings, 97th Congress, 2d session. Sept. 18, 19; Nov. 19; Dec. 9, 1981. Washington: U.S. Govt. Print. Off.; 1982. 678 p.

———*DOE coal-conversion orders to electric utilities, including the Long Island Lighting Company.* Hearings, 96th Congress, 2d session. Feb. 28, 1980. Washington: U.S. Govt. Print. Off.; 1980. 209 p. "No. 117" LRS80-8101.

U.S. Congress. Senate. Committee on Energy and Natural Resources. *Acid precipitation and the use of fossil fuels.* Hearings, 97th Congress, 2d session. Aug. 19, 1982. Washington: U.S. Govt. Print. Off.; 1982. 1537 p.

———*Effects of acid rain.* Hearing, 96th Congress, 2d session, on the phenomenon of acid rain and its implications for a national energy policy. Part 1. May 28, 1980. Washington: U.S. Govt. Print. Off.; 1980. 752 p. "Publication no. 96-126" LRS80-12176.

U.S. Congress. Senate. Committee on Environment and Public Works. *Acid rain: a technical inquiry.* Hearings, 97th Congress, 2d session. May 25 and 27, 1982. Washington: U.S. Govt. Print. Off.; 1982. 848 p.

———*Hearing, 97th Congress, 1st session, on S. 1706, S. 1709, and S. 1718 to amend Clean Air Act to protect against acid rain and to control interstate pollution.* Washington: U.S. Govt. Print. Off.; 1982. 787 p. "Serial no. 97-H30" Hearing held Oct. 29, 1981.

U.S. Congress. Senate. Committee on Environment and Public Works. Subcommittee on Environmental Pollution. *Environmental effects of the increased use of coal.* Hearings, 96th Congress, 2d session. Washington: U.S. Govt. Print. Off.; 1980. 453 p. "Serial no. 96-H45" Hearings held Mar. 19-Apr. 24, 1980, LRS80-8524.

U.S. Congress. Senate. Select Committee on Small Business and the Committee on Environment and Public Works. *Economic impact of acid rain.* Joint hearings, 96th Congress, 2d session. Sept. 23, 1980. Washington: U.S. Govt. Print. Off.; 1980.

U.S. Congress. Senate. Committee on Environment and Public Works. *Clean Air Act Amendments of 1982.* Report 97-666, 97th Congress, 2d session. Washington: U.S. Govt. Print. Off.; 1982. 191 p.

Information Sources for Semiconductor Technology

Charles W. Moulton

ABSTRACT. The various types of information sources available to scientists and engineers interested in semiconductors are described, with emphasis on the interdisciplinary nature of this area. Illustrations of the pertinent primary and secondary information sources are given, and mention is made of specialized information and data centers.

INTRODUCTION

While the subject of semiconductors and semiconductive devices can be regarded from a number of different perspectives—semiconductivity and related physical properties as fundamental phenomena; semiconductors as materials; and device design, operation, and applications—the boundaries of these areas have become so blurred that it is axiomatic that those who work in this field need to approach it on an interdisciplinary basis. Research on semiconductors reaches into many areas beyond electronics—optics, electrochemistry, and catalysts, for example.

Various types of information sources for semiconductors are considered here, mainly from the standpoint of informing scientists of those disciplines that deal with the solid state in general and semiconductors in particular about the wide diversity of materials

---

The author is a senior editor at Chemical Abstracts Service, P.O. Box 3012, Columbus, OH 43210. He holds the PhD and MS degrees in physical chemistry from the University of Pennsylvania and the BS in chemistry from the University of Chattanooga.

The author thanks Mr. Robert S. Tannehill, Jr., who provided valued and appreciated suggestions during the preparation of this paper.

© 1984 by The Haworth Press, Inc. All rights reserved.

available on this subject. This information is of interest to chemists, ceramists, metallurgists, chemical and electrical engineers, and physicists.

Since the literature on semiconductors is so voluminous, no discussion of this type can hope to be exhaustive. At best, this paper can serve to indicate the broad scope of the subject and to point out the types of sources that might be considered for inclusion in library collections.

PRIMARY LITERATURE

Journals

There are today almost 8500 primary journals that publish papers on semiconductors. This figure approximates the number of periodicals that Cambridge Scientific Abstracts covers for its secondary journal *Solid State Abstracts.* Most journals concerned with the solid state contain semiconductor papers.

In a 1976 study, Hawkins[1] analyzed 91 primary journals in terms of their contents of semiconductor papers. Eighteen that he identified as core journals are listed in Table I. Eight of these journals published 50% of their papers on semiconductors, while the remaining ten devoted at least 30% to this area. (The listing has now expanded to 20 as a result of the recent divisions of the *Japanese Journal of Applied Physics* and *Physica Status Solidi.)*

Of the 18 titles in Hawkins' list, eight pertain to physics, three to chemistry and materials, and seven to engineering (including devices and applications). While the choice of the INSPEC databases (referred to as *Science Abstracts A* and *B* in his paper) for sampling biased the results somewhat toward physics and engineering, this distribution seems to be fairly representative of the types of journals in which such papers appear.

Conference Proceedings and Technical Reports

Significant portions of the primary literature on semiconductors are to be found in sources other than primary journals (43% in Hawkins' study). It is not uncommon for the proceedings of conferences and symposia to appear in print either as individual publications or as regular issues of or supplements to established jour-

Table I

Semiconductor Core Journals

Applied Physics Letters. CODEN APPLAB. ISSN 003-6951.

Fizika i Tekhnika Poluprovodnikov (Leningrad). CODEN FTPPA4. ISSN 0015-3222.
   English translation: Soviet Physics-Semiconductors. CODEN SPSEAX. ISSN 0038-5700.

Fizika Tverdogo Tela (Leningrad). CODEN FTVTAC. ISSN 0367-3294. English
   translation: Soviet Physics-Solid State. CODEN SPSSA7. ISSN 0584-5807.

IBM Journal of Research and Development. CODEN IBMJAE. ISSN 0018-8646.

IEEE Journal of Solid-State Circuits. CODEN IJSCBC. ISSN 0018-9200.

IEEE Transactions on Electron Devices. CODEN IETDAI. ISSN 0018-9383.

Japanese Journal of Applied Physics. Part 1: CODEN JAPNDE. Part 2: CODEN
   JAPLD8. ISSN 0021-4922.

Journal of Applied Physics. CODEN JAPIAU. ISSN 0021-8979.

Journal of Electronic Materials. CODEN JECMA5. ISSN 0361-5235.

Journal of Non-Crystalline Solids. CODEN JNCSBJ. ISSN 0022-3093.

Journal of the Electrochemical Society. CODEN JESOAN. ISSN 0013-4511.

Lietuvos Fizikos Rinkinys (variant title Litovskii Fizicheskii Sbornik). CODEN
   LFRMA7. ISSN 0024-2969.

Microelectronics Journal. CODEN MICEB9. ISSN 0026-2692.

Physica Status Solidi. A: Applied Research. CODEN PSSABA. ISSN 0031-8965.
   B: Basic Research. CODEN PSSBBD. ISSN 0370-1972.

Physical Review B: Condensed Matter. CODEN PRBMDO. ISSN 0163-1829.

Solid State Communications. CODEN SSCOA4. ISSN 0038-1098.

Solid-State Electronics. CODEN SSELA5. ISSN 0038-1101.

Solid State Technology. CODEN SSTEAP. ISSN 0038-111X.

nals. The proceedings of conferences that meet regularly may take on the nature of serial publications. However, some of the material presented at conferences and society meetings may be published after lapses in time, or may appear in print only in the form of abstracts of papers appearing on the programs.

Technical reports, many of which describe government-sponsored research, also enter the open (i.e., unclassified) literature outside of the normal journal publication system.

In addition to announcements, such as publishers' catalogs and reviews and other listings that appear in primary journals, society organs, trade publications, etc., the conference and report literature is cited in both the broadly-based secondary sources (e.g., *Engineering Index, Chemical Abstracts,* and those that devote themselves to this type of literature. Examples of the latter are Cambridge Scientific Abstract's *Conference Papers Index* and *Government Reports Announcements and Index,* published by the U.S. National Technical Information Service (NTIS). By serving as a source of this information, the information and data centers described below also provide a valuable service.

Patents

Large numbers of patent specifications are filed and issued each year on semiconductive materials and devices. For the search term SEMICOND:, there are 8800 postings with the entry year 1982 in Derwent's online database *World Patents Index.*

It is vital for libraries associated with corporate laboratories in particular to monitor this type of literature on a regular basis. As with the conference and report literature, patents are cited not only by the general secondary sources, but also by specialized ones; examples of the latter are *World Patents Index,* INPADOC, the CLAIMS databases produced by IFI/Plenum, the current-awareness bulletin *Current Energy Patents* published by the U.S. Department of Energy, and various national patent gazettes.

Reference Material

The outpouring of papers reporting research on semiconductors leads inevitably to the appearance of large numbers of monographs, annual reviews and "advances," and other specialized reference works dealing with all areas of the solid-state sciences. These come not only from those publishers who specialize in science and technology (e.g., Academic Press, Elsevier, McGraw-Hill, North-Holland, Pergamon, Springer-Verlag), but also from the technical societies and the university presses.

Although much of this material may be outdated fairly quickly because of the rapid progress of technology, there is a body of standard reference works that should be considered for representation in library collections. The following list of references is suggested:

(a) *American Institute of Physics Handbook*[2]—definitions, data, tables, and formulas for physics;
(b) *Constitution of Binary Alloys*[3]—phase diagrams of binary systems, mainly metallic;
(c) *Encyclopaedic Dictionary of Physics*[4]—a multivolume encyclopedia, with occasional updating supplements;
(d) *Encyclopedia of Physics*[5]—a single volume, with extended discussions of major topics in physics;
(e) *Handbook of Chemistry and Physics*[6]—data tables, with annual editions;
(f) *Handbook of Materials Science*[7]—physical properties of solids in particular;
(g) *Handbook of Physics*[8]—a comprehensive one-volume descriptive source on all aspects of physics;
(h) *Handbook of Tables for Applied Engineering Sciences*[9]—data tables;
(i) *International Tables for X-Ray Crystallography*[10]—the standard tables for x-ray diffractometry;
(j) *Lange's Handbook of Chemistry*[11]—definitions, data tables, and formulas for chemistry;
(k) *Methods of Experimental Physics*[12]—an extensive multivolume work on methods in physics;
(l) *Phase Diagrams for Ceramists*[13]—mainly oxide systems, with frequent supplements;
(m) *Phase Diagrams: Materials Science and Technology*[14]—a five-volume compilation on inorganic systems, including metals, ceramics, electronic materials;
(n) *Physical Chemistry: An Advanced Treatise*[15]—a definitive multivolume reference;
(o) *Treatise on Solid State Chemistry*[16]—a seven-volume set on the structure, properties, and chemical dynamics of solids

SECONDARY SOURCES

Abstracting and Indexing Services

There is a wide diversity among the abstracting services that cover one or another segment of the vast scientific and technological literature on semiconductors. Table II lists 16 of the principal abstract journals in this area.

There is considerable overlap in coverage by the secondary services. All of Hawkins' core journals are cited in databases as di-

Table II

Abstract Journals

Title	Publisher	Comments on Content
Atomindex	INIS	nuclear science & technology
Central Patents Index	Derwent	chemical patents
Chemical Abstracts	CAS	chemistry, physics, metallurgy
Current Physics Index	AIP	physics
Electrical and Electronics Abstracts	INSPEC	electronics
Electrical Patents Index	Derwent	electrical, electronic patents
Electronics and Communications Abstracts Journal	CSA	electronics
Energy Information Abstracts	EIC	electric power, solar energy
Energy Research Abstracts	DOE	reports generated by DOE, other federal agencies
Engineering Index	Ei	engineering, physics
Government Reports Announcements and Index	NTIS	unclassified reports from federally funded research
Metals Abstracts	MI	metal science, metallurgical engineering
Physics Abstracts	INSPEC	physics
Science Research Abstracts Journal	CSA	physics, quantum electronics
Scientific and Technical Aerospace Reports	NASA	space science, electronics
Solid State Abstracts	CSA	solid-state science

(N.B. For this and subsequent tables, publishers, database producers, etc., are identified more completely in the Appendix.)

verse as those of CAS and INSPEC, and all but one in that of *Ei*. However, these various services complement one another in terms of varying emphasis and degree of detail included, both in abstract content and in the depth of indexing. A paper on the physical properties of a semiconductive material is treated according to somewhat different approaches by those secondary services that direct themselves primarily toward chemistry, physics, or engineering. Some segments of the primary literature, because of the highly specialized nature or the relative obscurity of the journals in which they appear, might be cited by only one of the secondary sources.

While a researcher will naturally tend to consider first a secondary service that relates most directly to his or her training, it is worthwhile to consult more than one service to ensure adequate retrieval of information that has been interpreted from various viewpoints or has appeared in primary sources not widely cited.

The abstracting services, in addition to their major publications, commonly issue an array of derivative information sources in a variety of formats: print, microform, and computer-readable magnetic tape. The major tape files of interest here are described below.

Many of the abstracting services also publish specialized current-awareness bulletins, selected from the material in the databases to meet the needs of particular groups of users. These repackaged "spin-off" publications might be based only on document titles, or they may also incorporate the abstracts that are carried in the parent secondary journals. Some examples of bulletins of this type appear in Table III.

Computer-Readable Files

For all of the abstract journals referred to above, there are companion machine-readable versions. While some of these files may correspond exactly to the printed products, they frequently contain additional data (e.g., index entries). Some are composites of the material published in more than one journal (e.g., INSPEC, WPI), while one (EMIS) has no counterpart in print.

Seventeen of these files are listed in Table IV. All contain information that bears on the subject of semiconductor technology.

Online Search Services

Although any discussion of the computer-based search services is somewhat beyond the scope of a paper having to do with information sources, it seems wise to include a mention of them, since they are necessary adjuncts to gaining access to the machine-readable files.

The major U.S.-based, general-purpose search systems, BRS, DIALOG, and ORBIT, provide access to the tape files referred to in the previous section. Some of these files are also accessible via the European-based systems DATA-STAR, ESA-IRS (also referred to as ESRIN or ESA-QUEST), INFOLINE, INKA, and QUESTEL; several of these are available in North America.

There are also a number of search services that are intended only for users within particular nations. Examples of these are the Canada Institute of Scientific and Technical Information, a branch of the

Table III

Current-Awareness Bulletins

TITLE	PUBLISHER
Title-based	
Chemical Titles	CAS
Conference Papers Index	CSA
Current Contents	ISI
Current Papers	INSPEC
NTIS Title Index	NTIS
World Patent Index	Derwent
Abstract-based	
CA Selects Crystal Growth Optical and Photosensitive Materials Solar Energy	CAS
Energy Abstracts	Ei
Energy Updates Current Energy Patents Solar Energy	DOE
Metals Digests Cleaning/Finishing/Coating New Technology	MI

Table IV
Computer-Readable Databases

Designation	Producer	Content
CA SEARCH	CAS	corresponds to Chemical Abstracts
CLAIMS	IFI/Plenum	U.S. chemical & electrical patents
COMPENDEX	Ei	corresponds to Engineering Index
Conference Papers Index	CSA	corresponds to printed journal
ELCOM	CSA	includes data from Electronics and Communication Abstracts Journal
EMIS	INSPEC	solid-state electronic materials
ENERGY (DOE)	DOE	includes data from Energy Research Abstracts
ENERGYLINE	EIC	corresponds to Energy Information Abstracts
INIS	INIS	corresponds to Atomindex
INPADOC	INPADOC	patent literature
INSPEC	INSPEC	includes data from Electrical and Electronics Abstracts and Physics Abstracts
METADEX	MI	corresponds to Metals Abstracts (with Alloys Index)
NASA	NASA	includes data from Scientific and Technical Aerospace Reports
NTIS	NTIS	includes data from Government Reports Announcements and Index
SCISEARCH	ISI	corresponds to Science Citation Index
SPIN	API	includes data from Current Physics Index
World Patents Index (WPI)	Derwent	includes data from Central Patents Index and Electrical Patents Index

National Research Council, and the Japan Information Center for Science and Technology.

The U.S. Department of Energy (DOE) and the U.S. National Aeronautics and Space Administration (NASA) both maintain federally-supported search systems. DOE/RECON provides access to a number of energy-related databases and NASA/RECON to those concerned with aerospace. Use of these systems is intended mainly for personnel of federal agencies and their contractors.

Two specialized systems that provide searches of chemical compounds in terms of their structures are CAS ONLINE, which is offered directly by CAS, and DARC, associated with QUESTEL. Both of these systems rely on the CAS structure files. Because of the growing interest in the electrical properties of polymeric conductors, as well as other organic and coordination compounds, these structured-based search systems should demonstrate an increasing importance for research on semiconductors.

Information and Data Centers

The information and data centers serve a more specialized purpose than do the more broadly-based abstracting services. They typically include in their holdings not only material selected from the publicly available primary literature, but also reports of limited availability, perhaps classified or proprietary. They commonly publish current-awareness bulletins in their fields of interest, as well as bibliographies, monographs, and compilations of numerical data, perhaps critically evaluated. And they will carry out specialized searches that are beyond the capabilities of other libraries.

Information might be provided by such centers to the scientific community in general, but in certain instances access is restricted to sponsors, such as members of trade organizations or industrial consortiums, or to agencies and contractors of governmental bodies.

Examples of such centers of interest are the following:

(a) Alloy Data Center (U.S. National Bureau of Standards, Materials Bldg., Room B150, Washington, DC 20234; telephone (301) 921-2917)—physical properties of metals, alloys, semimetals, intermetallic compounds;

(b) Crystal Data Center (U.S. National Bureau of Standards, Materials Bldg., Room A221, Washington, DC 20234; telephone (301) 921-2950)—crystallographic data on metals, inorganic and organic compounds;

(c) Metals and Ceramics Information Center (Battelle Memorial Institute, Columbus Laboratories, 505 King Ave., Columbus, OH 43201; telephone (614) 424-5000)—physical properties and design characteristics of metals and ceramics, intended especially for military systems;

(d) Thermophysical and Electronic Properties Information Analysis Center (Purdue University, Center for Information and Numerical Data Analysis and Synthesis, 2595 Yeager Rd., West Lafayette, IN 47906; telephone (317) 463-1581)[17]—

thermophysical, electronic, electrical, magnetic, and optical properties of materials.

The U.S. National Bureau of Standards (NBS), through its Office of Standard Reference Data (Physics Bldg., Room A320, Washington, DC 20234; telephone (301) 921-2467), also coordinates a network of some 20 data centers and data-compilation projects, the National Standard Reference Data System (NSRDS). The purpose of this system is to provide critically evaluated numerical data on the physical and chemical properties of materials. NSRDS publishes several series of reports, and also has the major responsibility for the *Journal of Physical and Chemical Reference Data* (CODEN JPCRBU, ISSN 0047-2899), a serial jointly published by the American Institute of Physics, the American Chemical Society, and NBS.

CONCLUSIONS

A wide diversity of information sources across the spectrum of disciplinary interests is available for the subject of semiconductors. The types of organizations that deal with semiconductors run the gamut from the academic on one hand to the production-oriented industrial on the other. Organizational orientation will largely dictate which services are suitable for any particular site. The material presented here should, it is hoped, provide help for those who must decide which services to select for library usage.

REFERENCES

1. Hawkins, D. T. Semiconductor journals. *Journal of Chemical Information and Computer Sciences.* 16(1): 21-23; 1976.

2. Gray, D. E., ed. *American Institute of Physics handbook.* 3rd ed. New York: McGraw-Hill; 1972.

3. Hansen, M. *Constitution of binary alloys.* 2nd edition. New York: McGraw-Hill; 1958 (with supplements compiled by Elliott, R. P.; 1965 and Shunk, F. A.; 1969).

4. Thewlis, J. [and others], eds. *Encyclopaedic dictionary of physics.* Oxford and London: Pergamon Press; 1971 et seq.

5. Lerner, R. G.; Trigg, G. L., eds. *Encyclopedia of physics.* Reading, MA: Addison-Wesley; 1981.

6. Weast, R. C., ed. *Handbook of chemistry and physics.* 63rd ed. Boca Raton, FL: CRC Press; 1982.

7. Lynch C. T., ed. *Handbook of materials science.* Boca Raton, FL: CRC Press; 1974 et seq.

8. Condon, E. U.; Odishaw, H., eds. *Handbook of physics*. 2nd ed. New York: McGraw-Hill; 1967.
9. Bolz, R. E.; Tuve, G. L., eds. *Handbook of tables for applied engineering sciences*. 2nd ed. Boca Raton, FL: CRC Press; 1973.
10. Lonsdale, K. [and others], eds. *International tables for X-ray crystallography*. Birmingham, UK: Kynoch Press; 1969 et seq.
11. Dean, J. A., ed. *Lange's handbook of chemistry*. 12th ed. New York: McGraw-Hill; 1979.
12. Marton, L., ed. *Methods of experimental physics*. New York: Academic Press; 1959 et seq.
13. Levin, E. M. [and others], eds. *Phase diagrams for ceramists*. Columbus, OH: American Ceramic Society; 1964 et seq.
14. Alper, A. M., ed. *Phase diagrams: materials science and technology*. New York: Academic Press; 1970-78.
15. Eyring, H.; Jost, W.; Henderson, D., eds. *Physical chemistry: an advanced treatise*. New York: Academic Press; 1972-79.
16. Hannay, N. B., ed. *Treatise on solid state chemistry*. New York: Plenum Press; 1973-1976.
17. Ho, Cho-Yen. *Center for information and numerical data analysis and synthesis*. NTIS Report AD-A100 772. 1981.
18. Ho, Cho-Yen. *Thermophysical and Electronic Properties Information Center: a continuing system program on data tables of thermophysical and electronic properties of materials*. West Lafayette, IN: Center for Information and Numerical Data Analysis and Synthesis; 1981; Final report (Jan. 1-Dec. 31, 1980); AD-A100 772/3.

BIBLIOGRAPHY

International Council of Scientific Unions. Committee on Data for Science and Technology (CODATA). *Inventory of data sources in science and technology*. Paris: United Nations Educational, Scientific and Cultural Organizations; 1982.
Ibid. *International compendium of numerical data projects*. New York: Springer-Verlag; 1969.
Connoly, F. [and others]. *Solid state physics literature guides*. New York: IFI/Plenum; 1972-1979.
King, D. W. [and others]. *Scientific journals in the United States*. Stroudsburg, PA: Hutchinson Ross Publishing Co.; 1981.
Malinowsky, H. R.; Richardson, J. M. *Science and engineering literature: a guide to reference sources*. 3rd ed. Littleton, CO.: Libraries Unlimited; 1980.
National Referral Center. *Directory of information sources in the United States: physical sciences, engineering*. Washington, D.C.: Library of Congress; 1971.
Oliver, M. R. The effect of growth on the obsolescence of semiconductor physics literature. *Journal of Documentation*. 27(1): 11-17; 1971 Mar.
Schmittroth, J., Jr., ed. *Encyclopedia of information systems and services*. 5th ed. Detroit: Gale Research Co.; 1983.
Williams, M. E. [and others]. *Computer-readable databases: a directory and data sourcebook*. White Plains, NY: Knowledge Industry Publications; 1982.

Appendix

Key to Secondary-Journal Publishers, Database Producers, and Search-System Suppliers

AIP	American Institute of Physics, 335 E. 45th St., New York, NY 10017
BRS	Bibliographic Retrieval Services, 1200 Route 7, Latham, NY 12110
CAS	Chemical Abstracts Service (American Chemical Society), P.O. Box 3012, Columbus, OH 43210
CSA	Cambridge Scientific Abstracts, 5161 River Rd., Bethesda, MD 20816
DATA-STAR	Radio Suisse Ltd., Schwarztorstr. 61, CH-3000 Berne 14, Switzerland
Derwent	Dewent Publications Ltd., Rochdale House, 128 Theobalds Rd., London WC1X 8RP, England
DIALOG	DIALOG Information Services, 3460 Hillview Ave., Palo Alto, CA 94304
DOE	US Department of Energy, Technical Information Center, P.O. Box 62, Oak Ridge, TN 37380
Ei	Engineering Information, Inc., 345 E. 47th St., New York, NY 10017
EIC	Environment Information Center, Inc., 48 W. 38th St., New York, NY 10018
ESA	European Space Agency, Information Retrieval Service, ESRIN, Via Galileo Galilei, C.P. 64, I-00044 Frascati, Italy
IFI/Plenum	IFI/Plenum Data Co., 302 Swann Ave., Alexandria, VA 22301
INFOLINE	Pergamon Infoline Ltd., 12 Vandy St., London EC2A 2DE, England
INIS	International Atomic Energy Agency, International Nuclear Information System, P.O. Box 100, A-1400 Vienna, Austria
INKA	Fachinformationszentrum Energie, Physik, Mathematik GmbH, D7514 Eggenstein-Leopoldshafen 2, Federal Republic of Germany
INPADOC	Internationales Patentdokumentations-Zentrum, Mollwaldplatz 4, A-1040 Vienna, Austria
INSPEC	Institution of Electrical Engineers, International Information Services for the Physics and Engineering Communities, Station House, Nightingale Rd., Hitchin, Herts. SG5 1RJ, England
ISI	Institute for Scientific Information, 3501 Market Ave., University City Science Center, Philadelphia, PA 19104
MI	Metals Information, American Society for Metals, Metals Park, OH 44073; The Metals Society of London, 1 Carlton House Terrace, London SW1Y 5DB, England
NASA	U.S. National Aeronautics and Space Administration, Scientific and Technical Information Branch, 600 Independence Ave., S.W., Washington, DC 20546

Appendix continued

NTIS	US Department of Commerce, National Technical Information Service, 5285 Port Royal Rd., Springfield, VA 22161
ORBIT	System Development Corporation, 2500 Colorado Ave., Santa Monica, CA 90406
QUESTEL	Télésystèmes (France Câbles et Radio), 40, Rue du Cherche Midi, F-75006 Paris, France

Pest Management Literature: Collection Development

Syed M. A. Khan

ABSTRACT. Weeds, insects, diseases, nematodes, rodents, birds and animals have been called "pests" when they cause an economic loss or create health and esthetic problems. Synthetic pesticides developed in World War II started keeping pests under control and increasing food production that brought about a higher standard of living. However, adverse environmental effects began to appear in some cases. The interaction between these two forces is bringing a healthy change in pest control strategies. This review of the pest management literature is from a collection development point of view, and an attempt has been made to present a balanced picture of growth and sound environment literature.

INTRODUCTION

This article is intended to (1) draw attention to the different types of publications and organizations involved, (2) provide enough information to access earlier material, (3) introduce the subject to those not familiar with the terminology through book titles and annotations as far as possible, and (4) show the likely direction in which research is heading.

Weeds, insects, diseases, nematodes, rodents, birds and animals have been designated "pests" under certain circumstances, chiefly when they cause an economic loss or create health and esthetic problems.

The coexistence and competition between human beings and pests is well documented in history. Archeologists have described it and

---

Mr. Khan is Assistant Professor, Life Science Library, Purdue University, West Lafayette, IN 47907. He has the BS degree in agriculture from A.P. Agricultural University (Hyderabad, India) and MS degrees in both Library Science and Horticulture from the University of Illinois.

© 1984 by The Haworth Press, Inc. All rights reserved.

even the holy books have discussed it. However, only since World War II, when synthetic pesticides were introduced, have we been able to control pests and increase food and livestock production and improve our standard of living. In this process, Entomology (science of insects and their control), Plant Pathology (science of plant diseases and their control), Weed Science (science of weeds and their control), etc., have been collectively referred to as Pest Management (study of pests and their control). Just as we started to have control over pests, controversy began too.

Dichloro-diphenyl-trichloroethane (DDT), which was credited with saving hundreds of thousands of lives from diseases like plague and malaria, in and after World War II, took years to show its adverse effects. Rachel Carson's classic book, *Silent Spring,* [1] drew attention to this problem most dramatically, and, by becoming a symbol of modern society's struggle against pollution, the book is a force to reckon with.

At least three elements contribute to the present practices and future direction of pest management. First, the role of pest control research in providing profits for farmers, urban users and manufacturers (including stock holders). Second, impact of the first on people's health and environment. The third is composed of the first and the second, plus the social, economic, political and moral implications of avoiding hunger in the world. The first and the second elements are the active ones and their literature is the subject of this article. These elements make a good example of the "checks and balances" that exist in our society. The third element is basically a reactive one or an arbitrator. Advocates of these elements have attained a certain degree of understanding which can be summed up in three words: INTEGRATED PEST MANAGEMENT.

The *Factbook of U.S. agriculture*[2] describes the current situation as follows:

> The nation's food and fiber needs are now being met by only a small portion of the total work force . . . (rest) provide goods and services that contribute to our high standard of living. This would not be possible without the methods to control many of the estimated 10,000 species of harmful insects, more than 1,500 diseases caused by fungi, 1,800 different weeds that cause serious damage to crop plants . . . Pesticides remain one of our major components in integrated pest management systems.

PLACE OF AGRICULTURE IN THE WORLD ECOSYSTEM

A brief review of literature on the place of agriculture in the total ecosystem will help in placing pest management in its proper perspective.

According to *Agricultural-food policy review: Perspectives for the 1980s,*[3] pesticide use now exceeds a million pounds annually—$3 billion, i.e., 3-4% of farmers' variable production costs. Nearly 60% of the 1978 expenditures for all pesticides was for herbicides to control weeds, about 30% was for insecticides, and less than 10% was for fungicides to control diseases. Crosson and Frederick's[4] review projects pesticide use in the U.S. in 1985 as 328.6 million kilos of active ingredients based on land-using technologies and 353.6 million kilos of active ingredients based on land-conserving technologies—both figures for baseline production. For high production the figures are 377.3 million kilos of active ingredients based on land-using technologies and 409.7 million kilos of active ingredients based on land-conserving technologies.

Before considering the literature of the first and second active elements discussed earlier, a glance at the literature of the third element will be appropriate. The following books have self-explanatory titles most of the time: *Distant hunger: agriculture, food, and human values,*[5] *Future dimensions of world food and population,*[6] *The world food problem,*[7] *Beyond the green revolution: the ecology and politics of global agricultural development,*[8] *Ecological principles for economic development,*[9] *Agricultural ecology: an analysis of world food production systems,*[10] *Food-climate interactions,*[11] *Ecoscience: population, resources, environment,*[12] *Environment: resources, pollution and society,*[13] *Food, energy and society,*[14] *Energy for world agriculture.*[15] All these books cover the topic from different angles, but to some extent they dwell on world population, resources, energy, economics, environment and, above all, food production to avoid hunger.

PEST MANAGEMENT LITERATURE

Literature coming out in the late 1970s and the 1980s is reviewed here as far as possible, except for some classic material or to discuss a specific topic which is best handled in earlier material. Reference sources, guides, bibliographies and other reviews cited cover most of the earlier material that is significant. Medical and veterinary aspects of pest management have not been covered.

Reference Sources

Blanchard, J. Richard; Farrell, Lois, eds. *Guide to sources for agricultural and biological research.* Berkeley, CA: University of California Press; 1981.

Chapter C entitled, "Crop protection-pesticides and pest control" by Ming-yu Li and chapter G entitled, "Environmental sciences" by Lois Farrell are most relevant. Governmental publications are covered well.

Lilly, G. P., ed. *Information sources in agriculture and food science.* London: Butterworths; 1981.

This British counterpart to the one above has these two relevant chapters: Chapter 10 entitled, "Weed biology, weed control and herbicides" by J. E. Y. Hardcastle and Chapter 11 entitled, Crop protection" by J. B. Ford and R. Whitbread.

Rudd, Robert L. *Environmental toxicology: a guide to information sources.* Detroit: Gale; 1977.

About half the material is pesticides or agricultural oriented, as could be expected in view of the author's status in this field.

Considine, Douglas M.; Considine, Glenn D., eds. *Foods and food production encyclopedia.* New York: Van Nostrand Reinhold; 1982.

Pest management, particularly by chemical means, is covered by experts. Terms are explained and there are hundreds of entries.

Parker, Sybil P., ed. *McGraw-Hill encyclopedia of environmental science.* New York: McGraw-Hill; 1980.

In this edition agriculture is covered from a total environment point of view.

Li, Ming-yu; Dohn, Judi. *Pesticides: a selected bibliography.* Davis, CA: University of California, Davis. Food Protection and Toxicology Center. Documentation & Information Service; 1975 June.

Government, universities and small presses are covered well.

Morris, Robert F. *Postharvest food losses in developing countries: a bibliography*. Washington, D. C.: National Academy of Sciences; 1978.

Since an estimated 40% of food losses are reported in some countries this is an important area for preventing losses due to pests.

Two U. S. Department of Agriculture (USDA) bibliographies (nos. 14 and 19 respectively of the Bibliographies and Literature of Agriculture Series) are good sources of information on pest control and pesticides from an economic point of view:

Osteen, Craig D.; Bradley, Edward B.; Moffitt, L. Joe. *The economics of agricultural pest control: an annotated bibliography, 1960-80*. Washington, D. C.: USDA Economics & Statistics Service; 1981 January.

Spinks, Thomas; Dahl, Dale C. *Inputs used in U. S. farm production: a bibliography of selected economic studies, 1950-1980*. Washington, D. C.: USDA Economics & Statistics Service; 1981 April.

Other bibliographies produced by government departments or agencies are:

Lance, J. C. *A pollution research bibliography 1970-1976*. Washington, D. C.: USDA Agricultural Research Service; 1977.

Pesticide degradation and pesticide mobility are covered here. *Pesticides in soil and water: an annotated bibliography*. Cincinnati, Ohio: U. S. Department of Health, Education, and Welfare. Public Health Service. Division of Water Supply and Pollution Control; 1964 September.

Copenhaver, Emily D.; Wilkinson, Benita K. *Movement of hazardous substances in soil: a bibliography*. Cincinnati, OH: U. S. Environmental Protection Agency. Municipal Environment Research Laboratory; 1969 August.

The second of this two-volume work is about pesticides.

Two publications of the United Nations—a bibliography and a guide to information sources are relevant for this article. These are:

Rodent pest: biology and control—bibliography 1970-1974. Rome: FAO; 1977; FAO Plant production and protection paper no. 7.

The Food and Agriculture Organization and the World Health Organization produced this bibliography jointly.

Information sources on the pesticide industry. New York: Unipub; 1974.

The United Nations Industrial Development Organization produced this as UNIDO guides to information sources no. 10.

Handbooks are an excellent source of information in scientific literature because of their valuable data that have been collected with great care and from a variety of sources. The contributors or editors or compilers of handbooks are generally very well known in their respective areas of expertise. Sometimes the publishers collect a team of scientists and editors to produce a given handbook which comes out at regular intervals. The following are some of the more pertinent ones:

Pimentel, David, ed. *CRC handbook of pest management in agriculture.* Boca Raton, FL: CRC; 1981.

A current state of the art review of literature with contributions from experts makes this three volume handbook the most comprehensive and interdisciplinary work on the entire subject under consideration. The main entries of each volume deserve a place in this review. *Vol. I:* Introduction; Estimated losses of crops and livestock to pests; Estimated losses without pesticides and substituting only readily available nonchemical controls; Environmental control of pests on crops; Environmental control of pests on livestock. *Vol. II:* Extent and quantities of pesticide used; Utilization of biological, cultural, and quarantine controls in crops; Methods of pesticide application; Biological pest control—insect pests; Biological pest control-plant pathogens; Biological pest control-weeds; Biological pest control-livestock pests; Bee pollinators and their problems; Human pesticide poisoning. *Vol. III:* Major types of pesticides—chemical nature, modes of action, and toxicity; Movement of pesticides in the environment and biodegradability; Pest management systems.

The work is full of data, figures, charts and references. An article by Gregory Shaner, entitled, "Genetic resistance for control of plant disease" cites 286 references.

Zimdahl, Robert L. *Weed-crop competition: a review.* Corvallis,

OR: Oregon State University. International Plant Protection Center; 1980.

This review has 586 references and lists over 100 studies of weed biology. It is directed towards scientists in developing countries.

Farm chemicals handbook. Willoughby, OH: Meister. Annual.

An essential purchase. New products, new formulations, new company names, current consumption data are found. "Pesticide dictionary" and "Plant food dictionary" are most important. "Buyer's guide," "Alphabetical list of farm chemicals, manufacturers and suppliers," and "Index to pesticide dictionary, buyer's guide and plant food dictionary" are the other sections. The name, structure, composition, formulation, application, action, and LD 50 (lethal dose that would kill 50% of a given population) for each chemical is available in this handbook.

Pesticide handbook (Entoma). College Park, MD: Entomological Society of America. Annual.

Similar to the one above, it has additional sources of information; contacts for more information; pesticide laboratories; poison control centers; formulations, active ingredients and application of insecticides; listings of acaricides, desiccants, fungicides, herbicides, nematicides, plant growth regulators, adjuvants, etc.; data on use, imports and exports; and other listings.

Worthing, Charles R., ed. *Pesticide manual: a world compendium.* 6th ed. Croydon, England: British Crop Protection Council; 1979.

This edition of a standard work devotes a page to each chemical. Wiswesser line-formula notation; molecular formula; code nos. given by manufacturers or WHO or USDA; common, trade and chemical names are standard indexes.

Wiswesser, William J., ed. *Pesticide index.* College Park, MD: Entomological Society of America; 1976.

Similar to the one above. CAS numbers from Chemical Abstracts; molecular formulas; Wiswesser line notations; numeric index, etc., make this fifth edition a useful tool.

Weed control manual. Wiloughby, OH: Meister. Annual.

This is produced by the producers of the *Farm chemicals handbook.* It is about weeds and herbicides in crops, fruits, vegetables, grasslands, water, etc.

Newton, Michael; Knight, Fred B. *Handbook of weed and insect control chemicals for forest resource managers.* Beaverton, OR: Timber Press; 1981.

Forest vegetation management and forest insect management sections are most important. Chemical and nonchemical means of control are covered. An appendix gives details on managing poisoning cases for different types of chemicals.

Horst, R. Kenneth. *Westcott's plant disease handbook.* 4th ed. New York: Van Nostrand Reinhold; 1979.

Cynthia Westcott's tradition has been upheld by Kenneth Horst in this edition. The most significant sections are: plant diseases and their pathogens; host plants and their diseases; garden chemicals and their application. All major diseases and most minor ones and their descriptions and control methods are covered.

Howritz, William, ed. *Official methods of analysis of the Association of Official Analytical Chemists.* 13th ed. Washington, DC.: Association of Official Analytical Chemists; 1980.

Chapters 6 and 29 of the 52 chapters in this edition of a standard source cover pesticides. The index is indispensable.

Fryer, J. D.; Makepeace, R. J., eds. *Weed control handbook.* Oxford: Blackwell. Editions and dates vary for the two volumes.

The British Crop Protection Council (BCPC) produces this comprehensive work and revises it regularly. Vol. 1, in its 6th edition, is dated 1977. Principles of weed control are covered by experts. Vol. 2, in its 8th edition, is dated 1978. Recommendations for weed control chemicals for crops, lawns, fruits, etc., are British in scope.

Conferences and Society Publications

Some organizational publications have already been introduced in the "Reference sources" section. More will be covered here from a non-reference point of view.

The National Academy of Science (US) publishes significant report literature as part of the deliberations of its committees of experts. Names of committees and titles of books are self-explanatory. Examples:

National Research Council. Commission on Natural resources.

Board on Agriculture & Renewable Resources. Committee on Impacts of Emerging Agricultural Trends on Fish & Wildlife Habitat. *Impacts of emerging agricultural trends on fish and wildlife habitat.* Washington, DC: NAS; 1982.

National Research Council. Commission on Natural Resources. Environmental Studies Board. Committee on Urban Pest Management. *Urban pest management.* Washington, DC: NAS; 1980.

National Research Council. Commission on Natural Resources. Environmental Studies Board. Committee on Prototype Explicit Analyses for Pesticides. *Regulating pesticides.* Washington, DC: NAS; 1980.

Laws, regulations, evaluations, adverse effects of pesticides are covered. Many governmental and outside bodies monitor pesticides.

National Research Council. Environmental Studies Board. Study on Problems of Pest Control. *Pest control: an assessment of present and alternative technologies.* Washington, DC: NAS; 1975.

This 5-volume work is a classic. The volumes are: Vol. I: Contemporary pest control practices and prospects: the report of the executive committee; Vol. 2: Corn/soybeans pest control; Vol. 3: Cotton pest control; Vol. 4: Forest pest control; and Vol. 5: Pest control and public health.

National Research Council. Assembly of Life Sciences. Division of Biological Sciences. Committee on the Effects of Herbicides in Vietnam. *The effects of herbicides in South Vietnam.* Washington, DC: NAS; 1974.

Part A—Summary and conclusions: This is one of the most authoritative independent studies conducted on the use of defoliants ("agent orange" for example) in Indo-China.

American Chemical Society's Division of Pesticide Chemistry publishes conference proceedings as the ACS Symposium Series. Examples:

Hedin, Paul A., ed. *Plant resistance to insects.* Washington, DC: ACS; 1983; ACS Symposium Series 208.

Moreland, Donald E.; St. John, Judith B.; Hess, F. Dana, eds. *Biochemical responses induced by herbicides.* Washington, DC: ACS; 1982; ACS Symposium Series 181.

Harvey, John, Jr.,; Zweig, Gunter, eds. *Pesticide analytical methodology.* Washington, DC: ACS; 1980; ACS Symposium Series 136.

Khan, M. A. Q.; Mann, J. J., eds. *Pesticide and xenobiotic metabolism in aquatic plants.* Washington, DC: ACS; 1979; ACS Symposium Series 99.

Paulson, Gaylord D.; Frear, D. Stuart; Marks, Edwin P., eds. *Xenobiotic metabolism: in vitro methods.* Washington, DC: ACS; 1979; ACS Symposium Series 97.

The ASTM Committee E-35 on Pesticides of the American Society for Testing and Materials (ASTM) publishes its proceedings as ASTM Special Technical Publications. These come out a bit late. Examples are:

Beck, J. R., ed. *Vertebrate pest control and management materials: proceedings of the second symposium on test methods for vertebrate pest control and management materials.* Philadelphia: ASTM; 1979; ASTM Special Technical Publication 680.
Rodents, birds and canine pests were the vertebrates considered.

Eaton, J. G.; Parrish, P. R.; Hendricks, A.C., eds. *Aquatic toxicology: proceedings of the third annual symposium on aquatic toxicology.* Philadelphia: ASTM; 1980; ASTM Special Technical Publication 707.

Lamb, D. W.; Kenaga, E. E., eds. *Avian and mammalian wildlife toxicology: second conference.* Philadelphia: ASTM; 1981; ASTM Special Technical Publication 757.

The British Crop Protection Council (BCPC) is a major publisher of pest management literature. Two of their most popular conferences conducted every other year attract hundreds of scientists from many countries. These are:

Proceedings of the 1982 British crop protection conference—Weeds. Croydon, England: BCPC; 1982.

Proceedings of the 1981 British crop protection conference—Pests and diseases. Croydon, England: BCPC; 1981.

Wright, E. N., ed. *Bird problems in agriculture: proceedings of a conference.* Croydon, England: BCPC: 1980, is another of the BCPC conference proceedings which is of interest.

The American Association for the Advancement of Science (AAAS) publishes its committees' proceedings as the AAAS Selected Symposium Series. An example is:

Pimentel, David; Perkins, John H., eds. *Pest control: cultural and environmental aspects.* Washington, DC: AAAS; 1980; AAAS Selected Symposium 43.

Social, economic, legal, environmental and technological aspects of pest control were covered.

The New York Academy of Sciences conducts many conferences whose proceedings are published as its annals. Examples of recent ones are:

Hammond, E. Cuyler: Selikoff, Irving J.; eds. *Public control of environmental health hazards.* New York: New York Academy of Sciences; 1979; Annals of the New York Academy of Sciences, Vol. 329.

Robert S. Jackson's article "Early testing and subsequent evaluation of the insecticide Kepone" concerns pesticides.

Day, Peter R., ed. *The genetic basis of epidemics in agriculture.* New York: New York Academy of Sciences; 1977; Annals of the New York Academy of Sciences, Vol. 287.

Two conferences conducted by the Federation of British Plant Pathologists and their proceedings, published by Blackwell of Oxford, are:

Jenkyn, J. F.; Plumb, R. T., eds. *Strategies for the control of cereal diseases.* Oxford: Blackwell; 1981.

Ebbels, D. L.; King, J. E., eds. *Plant health: The scientific basis for administrative control of plant disease and pests.* Oxford: Blackwell; 1981.

The Scientific Committee on Pesticides of the International Association on Occupational Health conducted the next two conferences whose proceedings were published by Elsevier. Titles are self-explanatory.

Tordoir, W. F.; Heemstra-Lequin, E. A. H., eds. *Field worker exposure during pesticide application: proceedings of the 5th international workshop.* Amsterdam: Elsevier; 1980.

Heemstra-Lequin, E. A. H.; Tordoir, W. F., eds. *Education and safe handling in pesticide application: proceedings of the 6th international workshop.* Amsterdam: Elsevier; 1982.

The next two conferences are about "semiochemicals" which are commonly known as pheromones or sex attractants for biological control.

Mitchell, Everett D., ed. *Management of insect pests with semiochemicals: concepts and practice.* New York: Plenum; 1981.

The conference was conducted by the Insect Attractants, Behavior, and Basic Biology Research Laboratory, USDA and the Dept. of Entomology and Nematology, University of Florida, Gainesville.

Nordlund, Donald A.; Jones, Richard L.; Lewis, W. Joe, eds. *Semiochemicals: their role in pest control.* New York: Wiley, 1981.

The book consists of papers selected from two conferences: a. "Recent advances in biological control technology. Interactions of entomologists and semiochemicals" (conference held with the 1978 Entomological Society of America meeting); b. "Behavioral chemicals: Role and employment in plant protection" (conference held with the 9th international congress of plant protection in 1979).

The following two books belong to the NATO advanced study institutes series of conference proceedings:

Lieberman, Morris, ed. *Post-harvest physiology and crop preservation.* New York: Plenum; 1983.

NATO, USDA, and the Greek Ministry of Agriculture jointly sponsored this symposium.

Wood, R. K. S., ed. *Active defense mechanisms in plants.* New York: Plenum; 1982.

Amongst others the National Science Foundation helped finance this symposium about the inherent defense mechanisms of crop plants against pests which the breeders have tried to exploit to evolve new strains of resistant plants that could withstand the pressure of pests.

Two American Phytopathological Society symposium proceedings are:

Erwin, D. C.; Bartnicki-Garcia, S.; Tsao, P. H., eds. *Phytophthora: its biology, taxonomy, ecology, and pathology.* St. Paul, Minnesota: American Phytopathological Society; 1983.
  A comprehensive account of this genus of plant-pathogenic fungi.
Schneider, R. W., ed. *Suppressive soils and plant disease.* St. Paul, Minnesota: American Phytopathological Society; 1982.

The book consists of revised manuscripts of a symposium entitled, "Nature of soils suppressive to soil-borne diseases." Some soils that suppress disease development although a pathogen is introduced in the presence of a susceptible host are being used to control plant diseases.

The Rockefeller Foundation's Bellagio Study and Conference Center in Italy draws renowned scientists who present state of the art and forward looking papers. Two such conferences produced these books:

Staples, Richard C.; Toennienssen, Gary H., eds. *Plant disease control.* New York: Wiley; 1981.
  This conference was jointly conducted with the Boyce Thompson Institute of Cornell University.

Metcalf, Robert L.; McKelvey, Jr., John J., eds. *The future for insecticides: needs and prospects.* New York: Wiley; 1976.
  This classic book brought changes in chemical control of insects.

Some other conference proceedings are:

Overcash, Michael R.; Davidson, James M., eds. *Environmental impact of nonpoint source pollution.* Ann Arbor, MI: Ann Arbor Science; 1980.
  EPA and the University of North Carolina supported this conference which covered water runoff from agricultural sources and related issues.

Shejbal, J. *Controlled atmosphere storage of grains.* Amsterdam: Elsevier; 1980.

Technical, economic, preservation quality, microbiological and entomological aspects of controlled atmospheric storage are covered.

Charudattan, R.; Walker, H. L., eds. *Biological control of weeds with plant pathogens.* New York: Wiley; 1982.
   Amongst others USDA helped organize this international workshop.

Del Fosse, E. S., ed. *Proceedings of the fifth international symposium on biological control of parasitic weeds.* Melbourne, Australia: Commonwealth Scientific and Industrial Research Organization; 1981.
   CSIRO conducts this series of conferences every 2-3 years from 1969. Musselman, L. J.; Worsham, A. D.; Eplee, R. E., eds. *Proceedings of the second international symposium on parasitic weeds.* Raleigh, NC: North Carolina State University; 1979.

Cutter, D. F.; Alvin, K. L.; Price, C. E., eds. *The plant cuticle.* London: Academic; 1981.
   This book is no. 10 in the Linnean Society Symposium Series. Since many plant growth regulators and pesticides are uptaken through the cuticle, the third part covered it and cuticle permeability as well.

The Center for Agricultural Publishing and Documentation, Wageningen, the Netherlands (Pudoc) is a major contributor to agricultural literature. Two of their conference proceedings are:

Heybroek, H. M.; Stephan, B. R.; von Wissenberg, K., eds. *Resistance to diseases and pests in forest trees: proceedings of the third international workshop on the genetics of host-parasite interactions in forestry.* Wageningen, the Netherlands: Pudoc; 1982.

Palti, J.; Kranz, J., eds. *Comparative epidemiology: a tool for better disease management—proceedings of the session on comparative epidemiology, third international congress of plant pathology.* Wageningen, the Netherlands: Pudoc; 1980.

The Commonwealth Agricultural Bureaux (CAB) and its associated bodies in Farnham Royal produce an enormous amount of information besides their famous abstracting series. The organization owned by the British Commonwealth countries is run on a no-profit no-loss basis. Some of their publications, though not conference proceedings, deserve listing. These are:

Descriptions of pathogenic fungi & bacteria (1964-)

Descriptions of plant viruses (1970-)

Distribution maps of pests. Series A: Agricultural (1951-)

Distribution maps of plant diseases (1942-)

Universities also conduct conferences on their own (not just sponsor them). Two examples are:

Holt, Harvey A.; Fischer, Burnell C., eds. *Weed control in forest management: proceedings, 1981 John S. Wright Forestry Conference.* West Lafayette, IN: Purdue University; 1981.

Hatfield, Jerry L.; Thomason, Ivan J., eds. *Biometeorology in integrated pest management.* New York: Academic; 1982. The University of California system, renowned for integrated pest management work, conducted this conference.

The Weed Science Society of America's publications of note are:

Herbicide handbook. 4th ed. Champaign, IL: Weed Science Society of America; 1979.
This is the latest edition of a standard work.

Adjuvants for herbicides. Champaign, IL: Weed Science Society of America; 1982.
Adjuvants are part of the formulations of pesticides and make them more effective.

Examples of publications of other societies are:

Christensen, Clyde M., ed. *Storage of cereal grains and their products.* 3d ed. St. Paul, MN: American Association of Cereal Chemists, Inc.; 1982.
Experts have contributed to this work.

Guenzi, W. D., ed. *Pesticides in soil and water.* Madison, WI: Soil Science Society of America; 1974.
Members of the society have contributed to this famous book.

Books by Major Publishers

In order to cover these books properly, it will be essential to discuss them from the point of view of the traditional breakdown of the pest management discipline point of view, i.e., Pesticides, Entomology, Nematology, Plant Pathology, Weed Science, etc. Some titles are self-explanatory and others will be annotated.

Ware, George W. *Pesticides: theory and application.* San Francisco: W. H. Freeman; 1983.

The author who writes similarly titled books every two or three years introduces the subject in clear and easy to understand manner.

Nickel, Louis G. *Plant growth regulators: agricultural uses.* Berlin: Springer-Verlag; 1982.

Synthetic plant growth regulators, like the famous 2, 4-D, that modify growth and development in the desired direction are covered.

Hartley, G. S., Graham-Bryce, I. J., eds. *Physical principles of pesticide behaviors: the dynamics of applied pesticides in the local environment in relation to biological response.* London: Academic; 1980.

Prominent scientists cover the subject thoroughly in two volumes.

Street, Joseph C., ed. *Pesticide selectivity.* New York: Marcel Dekker; 1975.

Pesticide selectivity is a most debatable topic. Are they target specific or non selective; are they broad spectrum or narrow spectrum—these are some of the issues covered in this important book. Broad spectrum pesticides cover many kinds of vegetation and are considered less expensive but environmentalists have grave reservations about them. Similar is the case of non selective pesticides. Drift and runoff problems and persistence of pesticides in the environment are covered.

Carderelli, Nate. *Controlled release pesticide formulations.* Boca Raton, FL: CRC; 1976.

These pesticides are considered environmentally more sound because of their shorter persistence and better effect due to slow release, which reduces the amounts used.

Khan, Shamat U. *Pesticides in the soil environment.* Amsterdam: Elsevier; 1980.

Behavior and fate of pesticides in soils, their effect on soil microorganisms and uptake and incorporation into plants and the food chain are covered.

Edwards, Clive A. *Persistent pesticides in the environment.* Boca Raton, FL: CRC; 1973.

This famous scientist and author of the other book, "Environmental pollution by pesticides" describes residues left in the environment from persistent pesticides—chiefly the organochlorine group of DDT, aldrin, dieldrin, etc., and their effects on plants, animals, etc.

White-Stevens, Robert, ed. *Pesticides in the environment.* New York. Marcel Dekker; 1971-77.

This extensive treatise has contributions from leading scientists. This 3-volume work (in 4 pieces) is the most comprehensive on the subject.

Chakrabarty, A. M., ed. *Biodegradation and detoxification of environmental pollutants.* Boca Raton, FL: CRC; 1982.

Ways to control toxicity of environmental pollutants (including pesticides) and make them biodegradable and not stable for longer durations is a topic of recent concern and the subject of this book.

Overcash, Michael R., ed. *Decomposition of toxic and nontoxic organic compounds in soils.* Ann Arbor, MI: Ann Arbor Science; 1981.

Pesticides and other agricultural chemicals are covered here.

Chambers, Janice E.; Yarbrough, James D., eds. *Effects of chronic exposures to pesticides on animal systems.* New York: Raven; 1982.

Effects from the subcellular to the organismic level are discussed.

Gosselin, Robert E.; Gleason, Marion N. *Clinical toxicology of commercial products: acute poisoning.* 4th ed. Baltimore: Williams & Wilkins; 1976.

This edition of this authoritative work includes first aid and emergency treatments, formulations, ingredients, therapeutics and other useful information. Pesticides are covered well, although a bit dated.

Vettorazzi, Gaston. *International regulatory aspects for pesticide chemicals.* Boca Raton, FL: CRC; 1979.
Pesticide toxicology, residues and regulations are reviewed.

Arbuckle, J. Gordon et. al. *Environmental law handbook.* Washington, D.C.: Government Institutes, Inc.; 1979.
Chapter 6 of this sixth edition by Marshal Lee Miller is entitled, "Federal regulation of pesticides."

Perkins, John H. *Insects, experts, and the insecticide crisis: the quest for new pest management strategies.* New York: Plenum; 1982.
A historical review of entomology & entomologists, and casual.

Barrons, Keith C. *Are pesticides really necessary?* Chicago: Regnery Gateway; 1981.
A biological scientist informs lay people of the need for pesticides and their relative safety.

van den Bosch, Robert. *The pesticide conspiracy.* New York: Doubleday; 1978.
The late van den Bosch, an authority on biological control, lashes out against hypocrisy in governments, industries and some fellow scientists. Lots of intimate details and insights provided against pesticides.

Whiteside, Thomas. *The pendulum and the toxic cloud: the course of dioxin contamination.* New Haven: Yale University Press; 1977.
An incident in Italy and use of dioxin contaminated defoliant 2, 4, 5-T ("Agent Orange") in Vietnam are covered here. (Note: The June 1983 meeting of the American Medical Association has taken issue with reporters for "witch-hunting" in reporting dioxin contamination hazards.

van den Bosch, Robert; Messenger, P. S.; Gutierrez, A. P. *An introduction to biological control.* New York: Plenum; 1982.
This is a revised edition of the 1973 book "Biological control" by the two senior authors who are now deceased. Use of natural enemies, predators, sterile partners, attractants, microorganisms etc., to control harmful pests is referred to as biological control.

Metcalf, C. L.; Flint, C. L.; Metcalf, R. L. *Destructive and useful insects: their habits and control.* 4th ed. New York: McGraw-Hill; 1962.
This edition of the book is actually a revision by R. L. Metcalf. It is a most authoritative work by a giant in the field.

Sill, Webster H., Jr. *Plant protection: an integrated interdisciplinary approach.* Ames, Iowa: Iowa State University Press; 1982.
Chemical and nonchemical means of controlling pests are described.

Flint, Mary Louise; van den Bosch, Robert. *Introduction to integrated pest management.* New York: Plenum; 1981.
Integrated pest management (IPM) utilizes appropriate chemical and nonchemical means of pest control with minimum environmental effects. This easy to read book takes a historical and philosophical approach.

Maxwell, Fowden G.; Jennings, Peter R., eds. *Breeding plants resistant to insects.* New York: Wiley; 1980.
Experts describe different perspectives of breeding for resistance.

Poinar, Jr., George O. *Nematodes for biological control of insects.* Boca Raton, FL: CRC; 1979.
Nematodes, themselves a common pest, are used here to control insects.

Dropkin, Victor H. *Introduction to plant nematology.* New York: Wiley; 1980.
Biology, identification, pathology, diseases caused and control of nematodes harmful to plants are the topics covered in this book.

Vanderplank, J. E. *Host-pathogen interactions in plant disease.* New York: Academic; 1982.
A most famous scientist describes his own book thus in the preface: "host-pathogen interaction underlies all infectious disease, thus this work is primarily for plant pathologists and plant breeders concerned with the control of diseases."

Fry, William E. *Principles of plant disease management.* New York: Academic; 1982.

A good introductory text to chemical and nonchemical control of plant diseases. Diagnosis, epidemiology and exclusion are also covered.

Scott, K. J.; Chakravorty, A. K., eds. *The rust fungi.* London: Academic; 1982.
Rusts, which cause more crop losses than other pathogens, are covered well from genetics and biochemistry of host/parasite relationships aspect.

Mount, Mark S.; Lacy, George H., eds. *Phytopathogenic prokaryotes.* New York: Academic; 1982.
Complex interactions between prokaryotes and plant hosts are covered.

Daniels, M. J.; Markham, P. G., eds. *Plant and insect mycoplasma techniques.* London: Croom Helm; 1982.
Insect vectors, culture methods, microscopic procedures and control measures are discussed but the book is not a laboratory manual.

Nyvall, Robert F. *Field crop diseases handbook.* Westport, CT: AVI; 1979.
A simple handbook.

Durbin, R. D., ed. *Toxins in plant disease.* New York: Academic; 1981.
Different aspects of plant pathogens known to produce toxins that play a role in pathogenesis are covered in a comprehensive manner.

Mathews, R. E. F. *Plant virology.* New York: Academic; 1981.
The second of this work covers all aspects of plant virology.

Palti, Josef. *Cultural practices and infectious crop diseases.* Berlin: Springer-Verlag; 1981.
Cultural methods, rotations, early or late planting are some of the practices adopted to avoid pests. These and other controls are covered.

Sharvelle, Eric G. *Plant disease control.* Westport, CT: AVI; 1979.
Hundreds of fungicides, diseases, methods of control are discussed.

Zadoks, Jan C.; Schein, Richard D. *Epidemiology and plant disease management.* New York: Oxford University Press; 1979.
Ecological and environmental aspects of the subject are covered.

Mulder, D., ed. *Soil disinfestation.* Amsterdam: Elsevier; 1979.
Mostly chemical, but physical and biological means of control are explained for soils which are storehouses of pathogens.

Krupa, S. V.; Dommergues, Y. R., eds. *Ecology of root pathogens.* Amsterdam: Elsevier; 1979.
Control measures with emphasis on nonchemical methods for fungi, bacteria, nematodes and other soil pathogens are outlined.

Horsfall, James G.; Cowling, Ellis B., eds. *Plant disease: an advanced treatise.* New York: Academic; 1977-1980.
This five-volume work written by experts, is an excellent contribution to the literature. The volumes are: Vol. 1: How disease is managed; Vol. 2: How disease developed in populations; Vol. 3: How plants suffer from disease; Vol. 4: How pathogens induce disease; and Vol. 5: How plants defend themselves.

Torgeson, Dewayne C., ed. *Fungicides: an advanced treatise.* New York: Academic; 1967-1969.
This two volume work does not easily get outdated in spite of the subject matter. Vol. 1: Agricultural and industrial applications; environmental interactions; Vol. 2: Chemistry and physiology.

Dekker, J.; Georgopoulos, S. G., eds. *Fungicide resistance in crop protection.* Wageningen, the Netherlands: Pudoc; 1982.
Insects resistant to DDT created a big furor. This book covers factors contributing to the build-up of a resistant pathogen population and the genetic and biochemical basis of fungicide resistance.

LeBaron, Homer M.; Gressel, Jonathan, eds. *Herbicide resistance in plants.* New York: Wiley; 1982.
Will new strains of weeds resistant to herbicides emerge, as in the case of insects? The book's contributors found little development of herbicide resistance thus far, a significant conclusion because more than half the pesticides used today are herbicides.

Fedtke, Carl. *Biochemistry and physiology of herbicide action.* Berlin: Springer-Verlag; 1982.

Effects of herbicides on the metabolism of higher plants, mode of action and use as metabolic inhibitors in plant physiological research (photosynthetic inhibitor diuron) are reviewed in this book.

Hatzios, Kriton K.; Penner, Donald. *Metabolism of herbicides in higher plants.* Minneapolis: Burgess; 1982.

Organic herbicides are particularly well discussed. The direction in which the field is moving can be gauged from the title of this book. Knowledge of degradation pathways, binding to plants, selectivity, and environmental effects will determine the fate of future pesticides.

Eagle, D. J.; Caverly, D. J. *Diagnosis of herbicide damage to crops.* New York: Chemical Publishing; 1981.

Photographs showing damage to crops from drift, overdose, persistence, uneven or late application of herbicides are very clear. Symptoms of damage by different groups of pesticides are covered.

Bover, Rodney, W.; Young, Alvin L. *The science of 2, 4, 5-T and associated phenoxy herbicides.* New York: Wiley; 1980.

A review of literature of the most controversial and heavily used group of pesticides which showed teratogenic effects in laboratory animals.

Ashton, Floyd M.; Crafts, Alden S. *Mode of action of herbicides.* 2nd ed. New York: Wiley; 1981.

This significant work provides basic information on the physiology and biochemistry of herbicides which is needed for improving their efficacy and for causing minimal adverse effects.

The next three books are written or edited by an aquatic botanist. The titles are self-explanatory.

Gangstad, Edward O. *Weed control methods for river basin management.* Boca Raton, FL: CRC; 1978.

Gangstad, Edward O., ed. *Weed control methods for public health applications.* Boca Raton, FL: CRC; 1980.

Gangstad, Edward O., ed. *Weed control methods for rights-of-way management.* Boca Raton, FL: CRC; 1982.

Mallis, Arnold, ed. *Handbook of pest control: the behavior, life history, and control of household pests.* Cleveland, OH: Franzak & Foster; 1982.

This sixth edition of the most well known book on the subject is a comprehensive collection on almost all types of household pests and their control. Most control measures described are chemical or preventive.

Government Publications

The U.S. government probably publishes more material than any other single body in the world. Only two departments and one agency of the federal government are barely covered in this review. Local and state governments and agricultural service stations are left out due to their rather limited geographic coverage. Indexing and abstracting services and bibliographies cited cover these types of publications well.

US Department of Agriculture (USDA) and its subdivisions publish many series and revise many important or dated titles. A few publications from 1979 to date are reviewed here:

The *"USDA handbook series"* is well established. No. 571 entitled, "Guidelines for the control of insect and mite pests of foods, fibers, ornamentals, livestock, households, forests and forest products" has over 700 pages (so are its earlier and later versions—nos. 554 & 584). No. 585 entitled, "Forest management chemicals: a guide to use when considering pesticides for forest management" is over 500 pages long. Others on Southern Pine Beetle, Douglas-Fir Tussock Moth, Gypsy Moth, Integrated Pest Management have 5-25 pages. A historic and heavily cited issue is No. 291 dated August, 1965—"Losses in agriculture."

USDA annual serials are also sources of current information. Examples are: *"Agricultural statistics"*—pesticide production, foreign trade, prices are given. *"Forest insect and disease conditions"*—published by the USDA Forest Service. *"List of intercepted plant pests"*—published by USDA Animal and Plant Health Inspection Service: Plant Protection and Quarantine Division.

Although USDA conducted or sponsored conferences were covered earlier, two are cited here to show current nonchemical control interest.

Allen, George E.; Ignoffo, Carlo M.; Jaques, Robert P., eds. *Microbial control of insect pests: future strategies in pest manage-*

ment systems-selected papers from NSF-USDA-University of Florida workshop. Gainesville, FL: University of Florida; 1979.

Papavizas, George C., ed. *Biological control in crop protection.* New Jersey: Allenheld & Osmun; 1981.

This is the fifth Beltsville Symposia in Agricultural Research conducted by the Beltsville Agricultural Research Center (BARC).

Another publication with USDA collaboration is:

Moore, Harry B. *Wood-inhabiting insects in houses: their identification, biology, prevention and control.* Washington, D.C.: USDA Forest Service and US Department of Housing and Urban Development; 1979.

One heavily cited report published by the US Department of Health, Education, and Welfare (HEW) is worth noting here. It is:

Report of the Secretary's Commission on pesticides and their relationship to environmental health. Washington, D.C.: USHEW; 1969.

This 677-page historic document has a 310-page index prepared for it by Sharon L. Valley of the Toxicology Information Program of the National Library of Medicine. Renowned scientists were members of the commission. The report is full of important information and data.

A few U.S. Environmental Protection Agency (EPA) publications are essential entries in a review like this. These are:

Reinbold, K.A. et. al. *Adsorption of energy-related organic pollutants: a literature review.* Athens, GA: USEPA. Office of Research and Development. Environmental Research Laboratory; 1979 August.

Pesticides are included in this review.

Unger, Samuel G. (The Tuolumne Corporation, California). *Environmental implications of trends in agriculture and silviculture.* Athens, GA: USEPA. Office of Research and Development. Environmental Research Laboratory; 1978 December.

Pesticides are included in this review.

Donigan, Jr. et. al. *User's manual for agricultural runoff management (ARM) model.* Athens, GA: USEPA. Office of Research and

Development. Environmental Research Laboratory; 1978 August.
Pesticides are discussed in this manual.

Smith, C. N. et. al. *Transport of agricultural chemicals from small upland piedmont watersheds.* Athens, GA: USEPA. Office of Research & Development. Environmental Research Laboratory; 1978 May.
Pesticides are a major concern of this report besides nutrients.

The next two publications are very significant and are cited often. Both are based on the same contract (no. 68-01-2608, MRI project no. 3949C.)

von Rumker, Rosmarie et al. *Production, distribution, use and environmental impact potential of selected pesticides.* Washington, D.C.: EPA. Office of Water and Hazardous Materials. Office of Pesticide Programs; 1975.

von Rumker, Rosmarie et al. *A study of the efficiency of the use of pesticides in agriculture.* Washington, D.C.: EPA. Office of Water and Hazardous Materials. Office of Pesticide Programs. Final Report; 1975 July.

One last U.S. govt. publication should be covered. It is: *"Environmental Quality"*, an annual report of the Council on Environmental Quality to the President, who in turn submits it to the Congress. In the 1980 report, chapter 3 on water quality and chapter 7 on natural resources discussed pesticides and pest management.

International Organizations' Publications

The Food and Agriculture Organization (FAO) and the World Health Organization (WHO) of the United Nations (UN) are involved in pesticides and pest management. They work jointly in many instances. FAO's publications issued in Rome are covered here. Some others are included in the reference sources section and the indexing and abstracting sources and online databases section. Many FAO publications are reports of committees or parts of series. The most pertinent series for this review is the *"FAO plant production and protection paper"* series. Examples are:

No. 6—Pest resistance to pesticides and crop loss assessment (1971–1981). 3 volumes.

No. 13—FAO specifications for plant protection products, 2d rev. ed. 1979.

No. 16—Rodenticides: analyses, specifications, formulations. 1979.

As part of this series, these two significant titles are complementary to each other: *"Pesticide residues in food—report"* and *"Pesticide residues in food—evaluations."* Annual.

"FAO census of agriculture," "FAO production yearbook" and *"FAO animal health yearbook"* are some other valuable sources of data publication series.

The *"FAO animal production and health paper"* series has some useful titles like:

No. 7 (revision 1)—The environmental impact of tsetse control operations, 1980. (This was prepared by the Dept. of Toxicology, Agricultural University, Wageningen, the Netherlands.)

The *"FAO agricultural services bulletin"* series has some pertinent issues like:

No. 38—Pesticide application equipment and techniques, 1979. (This was prepared by the Agricultural Engineering Dept., University of California, Davis.)

FAO's work on the devastating desert locusts is also significant. Another standard work of FAO which is continuously updated is: *Crop loss assessment methods.* L. Chiarappa issued its third supplement in 1981. The original manual and all supplements go together.

Periodicals/Journals

Many serials have been covered so far. A few journals are listed here without annotations since most of them are well established. Some of the interdisciplinary journals like *Agronomy Journal, Crop Science, American Journal of Agricultural Economics* are not listed. These journals are listed as mere examples:

Annals of Applied Biology
Annual Review of Entomology

Annual Review of Phytopathology
Archives of Environmental Contamination and Toxicology
Ecological Entomology (former title: *Transactions of the Royal Entomological Society of London)*
Ecotoxicology and Environmental Safety
Entomophaga: A Journal of Biological and Integrated Control
Environmental Entomology
Environmental Pollution. Series A: Ecological and Biological (since the split in 1980, Series A is more pertinent).
Environmental Science and Technology
Farm Chemicals
International Pest Control
Journal of Economic Entomology
Journal of Environmental Science and Health. Section B: Pesticides, Food Contaminants, and Agricultural Wastes
Journal of Pesticide Science
Pest Control
Pesticide Biochemistry and Physiology
Pesticide Science
Phytopathology
Plant Disease: An International Journal of Applied Plant Pathology (former title: *Plant Disease Reporter)*
Plant Pathology
Tropical Pest Management (former title: *PANS*)
Weed Research
Weed Science
Weeds Trees and Turf

The following irregular serial publications or proceedings of the regional meetings are listed as examples of those kinds of material:

Analytical Methods for Pesticides and Plant Growth Regulators
North Central Weed Control Conference. *Proceedings*
Western Society of Weed Science. *Research Progress Report*
Residue Reviews: Residues of Pesticides and Other Contaminants in the Total Environment.

Indexing and Abstracting Sources and Online Databases

To keep up with the current research publications, indexes and abstracts and their online counterpart databases are very helpful. Some of the more pertinent ones are covered here.

Agrindex. Rome: FAO; 1975–. Monthly. Information in this system is input by cooperating centers in different countries and regions of the world. Therefore, it is unique in many respects. It is not much used here probably because of the other well established sources and because of lack of familiarity with the types of publications issued by many countries. It is very good for pest literature of those countries.

Bibliography of Agriculture. Phoenix, Arizona: Oryx; 1975–. Monthly. It started in 1942 but changed publishers. North American and state agricultural publications are covered well, although it is world-wide in coverage. Along with the National Agricultural Library Catalog (its monographic counterpart), it provides most of the information received at the National Agricultural Library (NAL). AGRICOLA is the online name for this source. CRIS database is available online only. Also produced by NAL, it covers research projects conducted or sponsored by USDA. NAL provides current awareness service to USDA employees (earlier land-grant institutions were also covered). The acronym for this is CALS. From its main database, NAL produces a series of bibliographies, the popular one being the "Quick bibliography series" on popular topics. NAL sends them free on request. They are announced in NAL's monthly newsletter, *"Agricultural Libraries Information Notes."*

Biological Abstracts and Biological Abstracts/RRM. Philadelphia: BIOSIS; 1926– (twice a month) and 1965– (twice a month), respectively. Between these two publications, biological and relevant agricultural literature is thoroughly covered. BIOSIS is its online name.

Biological Abstracts/RRM is only an index not an abstracting source. "Biosystematic index," "Generic index," and "Concept index" are unique features. *"Abstracts of entomology"* and *"Abstracts on Health Effects of Environmental Pollution"* are two of its subfiles relevant to this paper. The physiological and pure sciences aspect of pest management are covered the best.

Commonwealth Agricultural Bureaux (CAB) Abstracts. Farnham Royal, England: CAB. CAB abstracts is the online name for this source. The print sources are split into many files produced by the different units of this organization. The online file can be searched as a whole or separately. The more directly pertinent print sections are: *"Helminthological abstracts. Series B—Plant Nematology"* (1932–quarterly); *"Plant Growth Regulator Abstracts"* (1975–

monthly). *"Review of applied entomology. Series A: Agricultural"* (1913-monthly); *"Review of Plant Pathology"* (1922-monthly); and *"Weed Abstracts"* (1952-monthly). There is some duplication with NAL's work in particular, which could cause considerable concern in some areas.

Chemical Abstracts. Columbus, OH: CAS; 1907-. Weekly. It is an excellent source for pesticides, formulations and patent material. The "Chemical substance index" (inclusive of its CAS registry no.), "Formula index," "Patent index," "Index guide" are its unique features. CA Search is its online name. Other online files are also available.

Environmental Periodicals Bibliography. Santa Barbara, CA: Environmental Studies Institute; 1972-. Six times a year. Published by a non-profit organization this index covers pest management and agricultural material better than most similar titles. Environmental bibliography is the online file's name.

Government Reports Announcements and Index. Springfield, VA: NTIS; 1946-. Twice a month. Literature produced from federal money is included in this index.

"EPA Quarterly Bibliography" and its 1970-76 cumulative counterpart also can be found here by and large. Its subfile, *"Agriculture and food,"* is relevant to this review. Pest management gets good coverage. NTIS is the online name of this index. The organization is known for its document delivery and other specialized services.

Index Medicus. Bethesda, MD: NLM; 1880-. Monthly. It has a long history of title and agency changes. It is a standard bearer for online searching systems. Its subfiles like the *Abridged Index Medicus"* or its controlled vocabulary, SDI services, bibliographies and reviews, etc., are well known. MEDLINE is the online name.

Monthly Catalog of United States Government Publications. Washington, D.C.: Government Printing Office; 1895-. Monthly. Various agencies and departments of the government publish material that gets indexed here. GPO monthly catalog is its online name. Its series and report index are very useful.

Pesticides Abstracts. Washington, D.C.: USEPA; 1968-. Monthly. Pesticides and their adverse effects are covered here. It is generally not very regular and most of the material indexed is not unique and can be obtained from some of the other sources described in this review.

Science Citation Index. Philadelphia: ISI; 1961-. Six times a year. This is a unique source for its interdisciplinary coverage and its renowned "Citation index." ISI is famous for its many revolutionary ideas including the weekly *"Current Contents."* Two of these are related to this review—agriculture and life sciences. Its online file is called SCI search.

Selected Water Resources Abstracts. Springfield, VA: NTIS; 1968–. Six times a year. This index is produced by the Water Resources Information Center which is a part of the U.S. Dept. of the Interior's Office of Water Resources. It is particularly good for water pollution aspects of agriculture as far as pest management is concerned. Water resources abstracts is its online name.

Two databases without their printed counterparts are *PESTDOC.* London: Derwent; 1968–. It is commercially available from SDC's "ORBIT" service. The acronym stands for "Pesticidal literature documentation;" and *NPIRS.* W. Lafayette, IN: Entomology Hall, Purdue University; 1982–. Many rapid changes are taking place in this service. It is now being made available through TYMNET by a contract with Martin Marietta Data Systems (MMDS). The main item is the EPA registration data for pesticides. Agreement with EPA is being worked out for EPA's tapes. More states are joining in. There are seven to date with California soon to join. The acronym stands for "National pesticide information retrieval system."

CONCLUSION

The above review indicates the following: (a) there is a brighter future for INTEGRATED PEST MANAGEMENT, (b) research is heading at an accelerated pace towards a better understanding of all physiological and biochemical processes involved, and (c) further advances in storage techniques should reduce post-harvest losses.

One last book can end this article appropriately:

Anglemyer, Mary; Seagraves, Eleanor R.; LeMaistre, Catherine, C. *A search for environmental ethics: an initial bibliography.* Washington, D.C.: Smithsonian Institution; 1980.

This book, published under the auspices of the Rachel Carson Council, Inc., lists 446 titles. The subject index lists only three under the heading "Pesticides." Two of them *(Silent Spring* and *The Pesticide Conspiracy)* are covered in this review. This improvement in environmental impact is a healthy and welcome sign for all parties involved in the controversial subject of pests.

REFERENCES

1. Carson, Rachel. *Silent spring.* Boston: Houghton-Mifflin; 1962.
2. *Factbook of U.S. agriculture.* (USDA Miscellaneous Publication No. 1063.) Washington, D.C.: USDA; 1981 November; (I.11 Pesticides and Integrated Pest Management).
3. USDA. Economics & Statistics Service. *Agricultural-food policy review: perspectives for the 1980's.* Washington, D.C.: US Government Printing Office; 1981, April; AFPR-4.
4. Crosson, Pierre R.; Frederick, Kenneth D. *The world food situation: resources and environmental issues in the developing countries and the United States.* Washington, D.C.: Resources for the Future; 1977; Research Report 6.
5. Nicholson, Heather Johnston; Nicholson, Ralph L. *Distant hunger: agriculture, food, and human values.* W. Lafayette, IN: Purdue University; 1979.
6. Woods, Richard G., ed. *Future dimensions of world food and population.* Boulder, CO: Westview; 1981.
7. *The world food problem: a report of the President's Science Advisory Committee.* Washington, D.C.: The White House; 1967 May.
8. Dahlberg, Kenneth A. *Beyond green revolution: the ecology and politics of global agricultural development.* New York: Plenum; 1979.
9. Dasmann, Raymond F.; Milton, John P.; Freeman, Peter H. *Ecological principles for economic development.* London: Wiley; 1973.
10. Cox, George W.; Atkins, Michael D. *Agricultural ecology: an analysis of world food production systems.* San Francisco: W.H. Freeman; 1979.
11. Bach, Wilfrid; Pankrath, Jurgen; Schneider, Stephen H., eds. *Food-climate interactions.* Holland: Reidel; 1981.
12. Ehrlich, Paul R.; Ehrlich, Anne H.; Holdren, John P. *Ecoscience: population, resources, environment.* San Francisco: W.H. Freeman; 1977.
13. Murdoch, William W., ed. *Environment: resources, pollution and society.* Sunderland, MA: Sinauer Associates; 1975.
14. Pimentel, David; Pimentel, Marcia. *Food, energy and society.* New York: Wiley, 1979.
15. *Energy for world agriculture.* Rome: FAO; 1979.

A Guide to Information Sources in Genetic Engineering

Melinda E. Saffer

ABSTRACT. Recent advances in genetic engineering, and especially recombinant DNA technology, have widespread applications to medicine and agriculture, and this impact has been felt by both basic research and industry. Coincident with the boom in biotechnology is the proliferation of new books, journals, and other adjunct literature. Librarians must make certain that their collections are adequate to the task of serving the scientist as well as the corporate manager. Monographs, periodicals, patents, abstracting and indexing services—manual and computerized—are discussed. A list of sources is included.

INTRODUCTION

The most revolutionary development in biology in recent years has been the advent of genetic engineering, or, more precisely, recombinant DNA technology. Genetic engineering is the term used to describe the introduction of new genetic material into a cell. It does not imply necessarily that the two molecules never join together in nature, since frequently genetic engineering is used to achieve quickly and in high yield a result which occurs only very rarely in nature. Genetic recombination is, in fact, the normal process of gene exchange in all living organisms. When applied to the new technology, however, the term is usually taken to mean the joining

---

Melinda E. Saffer is the Library Director at the Worcester Foundation for Experimental Biology, 222 Maple Avenue, Shrewsbury, MA 01545, and holds degrees from Clark University and Simmons College (MLS). The author wishes to thank Ms. Dawn Renear of Integrated Genetics for her assistance and cooperation.

© 1984 by The Haworth Press, Inc. All rights reserved.

together of two DNA molecules in a test tube and the subsequent insertion of this "recombinant" molecule into a living system.[1] The practical consequences of recombinant DNA technology are far-reaching. Its most profound effects will be in the field of medicine, especially in the prevention of genetic disease, but in the long term, plant and animal breeding will also benefit.[2]

For more background on the subject, H.F. Judson's book, *The Eighth Day of Creation* is a highly readable history of the science of molecular biology. Along with comprehensible explanations of the science, Judson provides insights into the personalities of the major scientists working in the field. Two papers which have appeared in *Scientific American* also provide a concise overview for the layman: the earlier one is titled "The Manipulation of Genes,"[3] and the second is "Genetic Engineering in Mammalian Cells."[4] *The DNA Story: A documentary history of gene cloning* by J.D. Watson and J. Tooze offers an absorbing account, both social and scientific, of the gene cloning controversy. The scientific background outlines the techniques for recombining DNA and identifying cloned genes. A large portion of the volume consists of documents collected from the last decade which reflect the concerns of the scientists who pioneered DNA research. The major steps in the development of Recombinant DNA technology are outlined in Table 1.[4]

Genetic engineering technology is a synthesis of the scholarship and methodology from several areas of the life sciences. Bacteriology, virology, microbiology, biochemistry, cell and molecular biology all contribute to the field, and the literature, naturally, reflects this diversity. Of course, it is not within the scope of this paper to supply an extensive list of publications. This has already been done by Joseph Menditto and Debbie Kirsch in their excellent bibliography, *Genetic Engineering, DNA, and Cloning: A bibliography in the future of genetics,* which covers both the monograph and periodical literature from 1970 to 1981. The intent, rather, is to highlight recent examples of the literature, and to function as a guide for the development of a collection with a genetic/biotechnology focus.

Within the past decade the amount of newly published information relating to genetic engineering has expanded rapidly. The growth in the number of biotechnology related companies is far exceeded by the number of new books, journals, and newsletters in the field. Many long-established publishing houses have been striving to provide researchers with important up-to-date laboratory techniques

TABLE 1: Major Steps in the Development of Recombinant DNA Technology

1869 -- DNA isolated for the first time.

1944 -- DNA proven capable of altering heredity in bacteria.

1953 -- Watson and Crick proposed the double-helix model for DNA structure.

1966 -- Establishment of complete genetic code.

1967 -- Isolation of DNA ligase, the enzyme used to join DNA fragments together.

1972 -- DNA cloning techniques developed at Stanford University.

1976 -- Release of first guidelines by National Institutes of Health and rising public concern over potential dangers.

1977 -- Formation of the first genetic engineering company (Genentech).

1980 -- The Nobel Prize in Chemistry is awarded for the cloning of the first recombinant DNA molecules and the development of powerful methods for sequencing DNA.

and authoritative information on recent developments. John Wiley and Sons offers a wide variety of textbooks and monographs which relate to genetic engineering. Academic Press publications range from recombinant DNA and monoclonal antibodies to fermentation science, enzymes, biomass, and plant genetics. Particularly noteworthy is their series *Methods in Enzymology,* which will be discussed later. Excellent biochemistry and molecular biology monographs and texts are published by Springer-Verlag and Verlag Chemie International. Addison-Wesley, well known for publishing fine university chemistry, physics and mathematics texts, has initiated a new series on biotechnology. Raven Press publishes many titles in genetics and related fields, several of which are conference proceedings. In addition to its annual *Symposium on Quantitative Biology,* Cold Spring Harbor also publishes a number of laboratory manuals, monographs, proceedings from the *Conferences on Cell Proliferation,* and the *Banbury Reports.*

The book review section of many periodicals is another source of recent titles—*Cell, Trends in Biochemistry, Trends in Biotechnology,* and *Biotechnology* all contain informative reviews, as do general science journals such as *Science, Bioscience, Quarterly*

Reviews of Biology, and especially the semi-annual book supplements of *Nature,* published in November and April.

TEXTBOOKS AND REFERENCE SOURCES

A few basic reference tools for a genetic engineering collection might include the *CRC Handbook of Biochemistry and Molecular Biology,* particularly Section B: Nucleic Acids, and the *CRC Handbook of Microbiology.* A recent British publication, *Biotechnology Made Simple: A glossary of recombinant DNA and hybridoma technology* is, as its name suggests, a dictionary of biochemistry and genetics. Other sections of this volume include an introduction to DNA recombination, monoclonal antibody techniques, and a series of tables of information ranging from nucleic acid nomenclature to methods of interferon production. Of potential interest to business managers and administrators is the *Genetic Engineering and Biotechnology Yearbook 1983.* This book is packed with information about companies and institutes throughout the world. The *Genetic Engineering/Biotechnology Sourcebook* identifies and describes 1,529 research projects, and is useful for pinpointing current research interests of specific investigators and organizations.

The collection should also include a general introductory biochemistry text with an emphasis on molecular genetics. Both the books by Lubert Stryer and Albert Lehninger are very reliable and well illustrated. Bruce Alberts' *Molecular Biology of the Cell* is chiefly concerned with eucaryotic cells, as opposed to bacteria. Intended for students taking a first course in cell biology, it also is useful to the working scientist as a reference source. The volume is exceptionally illustrated and the list of references extensive. Arthur Kornberg's *DNA Replication* is an up-to-date account of replication and metabolism with a strong biochemical emphasis which can be used both for orientation to the subject and also as an information resource. A supplement to the volume was published in 1982 and "cites items and key references that alert the reader to important developments from June 1979 to January 1982." Also noteworthy for its comprehensive account of the problems of DNA sequence data analysis is *Statistical Analysis of DNA Sequence Data* by B.S. Weir. All types of DNA data and statistical methodologies are indexed, and available computer programs are surveyed. No library with a focus on DNA would be complete without J.D. Watson's

Molecular Biology of the Gene, an authoritative and detailed coverage of the subject.

LABORATORY MANUALS AND METHODOLOGY

A common variation on the basic textbook is the laboratory manual. These methodology texts are directed at the practitioner rather than the student. A series by T.S. Work titled *Laboratory Techniques in Biochemistry and Molecular Biology* is a particularly good overview of various methods frequently employed in the field. *Molecular Cloning: A laboratory manual* by T. Maniatis contains a description of the principles of cloning and detailed protocols for all the fundamental techniques currently in use. Numerous illustrations, comprehensive appendixes, a complete bibliography, and a detailed index enhance the design for use on the lab bench. Other manuals available from Cold Spring Harbor are *Advanced Bacterial Genetics,* containing general information on experimental protocols and many specific recipes, with special emphasis on new genetic approaches and recombinant DNA technology; *Hybridoma Techniques* covers the preparations of medium constituents, cloning, large-scale production of monoclonal antibodies, etc. Also useful is *Practical Methods in Molecular Biology* by R.F. Schlief and P.C. Wensink. This book contains a large number of techniques relevant to genetic engineering. Methods are described for DNA purification, concentration, and quantification as well as some procedures necessary for cloning genes from higher organisms. *DNA Repair: A laboratory manual of research procedures* presents numerous methodologies in cookbook detail—two volumes are presently available. Other methodology books worthy of note include Jeffrey Miller's *Experiments in Molecular Genetics;* and D.M. Glover's *Genetic Engineering; Cloning DNA,* a brief 80 page summary of techniques. Finally, the series *Methods in Enzymology* is an invaluable source. Published six to nine times a year by Academic Press, it provides researchers with precise methodology for executing a variety of current laboratory techniques. The entire series is directed at those performing the research, from the principle investigator to laboratory technical personnel. It is a true "methods" series, in that it includes almost every detail from basic theory to sources of equipment and reagents, with timely documentation provided on each page. Of particular interest are vol. 65: Nucleic Acids, edited by Lawrence

Grossman and Kivie Moldave; vol. 68: Recombinant DNA, edited by Ray Wu; and vols. 100 and 101: Recombinant DNA, Parts B & C, edited by Ray Wu, Lawrence Grossman and Kivie Moldave.

PERIODICAL LITERATURE

Any survey of the reading habits of scientists will reveal that periodicals are the most frequently used sources of information. Publishers are launching new journals at an exponential rate, so it is not surprising that the genetic engineering boom has struck the periodical literature as well as the book literature. The proliferation of research and the huge expansion of technology have triggered a need for journals specific to genetic and recombinant DNA technology. These can be divided into two categories: the original research journal, and the news and information journal.

Of the recent crop of research journals many seem to favor the rapid communication format—*Journal of Molecular and Applied Genetics* publishes full-length articles on studies utilizing modern genetic techniques, especially recombinant DNA methods, to solve basic and applied problems in genetics, biochemistry, medicine, and agriculture; *Gene* focuses on gene cloning, structure, and function, and includes papers on biochemicals methods; *DNA Repair Reports* is a new section of *Mutation Research,* but may also be purchased separately. *DNA: A Journal of Molecular Biology,* started in 1982, publishes research papers, short communications, reviews, technical notes, and editorials on any subject dealing with eucaryotic or procaryotic gene structure, organization, expression, and evolution. Others with an emphasis in the field are: *Molecular and General Genetics, Genetics, Genetical Research, Plasmids, Human Genetics,* and *Biochemical Genetics.*

There are now some 30 publications that provide, in one way or another, rapid information on biotechnology, with more appearing almost weekly.[6] These can be grouped into three types: the magazine format, the abstracting service, and the newsletter. *Applied Genetics News, Biotechnology News, Genetic Engineering News,* and *Bioengineering News* are four very good variant clones of the general biotechnology newsletter. The titles of most similar publications can be constructed by permutations on these four titles—likewise the contents. Each covers recent discoveries, company news and patents, new key references, conferences, meetings, and courses. The discussion of each topic covers only one or two paragraphs, and there is an attempt at the use of headlines to catch the eye. The style is readable and the text informative. *Biotechnology Law Report* is aimed at a more narrow audience, dealing with patent law, regulatory, liability and biomedical law, tax securities, contracts and licenses—all as they apply to biotechnology. The magazine format is most conspicuously represented by the monthly journal from the publishers of *Nature*. Each issue of *Biotechnology* features three to six research papers, a review article, international news and industry profiles. Also included is a listing of recently awarded grants from the National Institutes of Health and the National Science Foundation, as well as a section on patents. Printed on glossy paper, the format lends itself to good quality photographs. A considerable proportion of the available space is devoted to large, multi-colored ads. The National Institutes of Health (NIH) publishes the *Recombinant DNA Technical Bulletin* quarterly. Although each issue contains one or two original scientific reports, the main emphasis is on news, meeting announcements, actions taken by NIH, and articles on public policy, law, and ethics. Each issue of the *Bulletin* also includes a set of citations to documents which discuss both technical and ethical aspects of recombinant DNA research. At present there are four major abstracting services of "newsy" material. *Abstracts of Biocommerce* is from IRL Press. It is a short, well presented publication confining itself largely to the commercial aspects of biotechnology and is presumably aiming at the business side of the scientific community. The coverage includes English language newsletters, British newspapers and some technical magazines. Patents and U.S. newspapers are not included. *Derwent Biotechnology Abstracts* provide a straight abstracting service in the broader context of biotechnology, including microbiology, biochemical engineering, chemistry and chemicals, pharmaceuticals, food agriculture, cell culture, energy, etc. No news or gossip, but, as would be expected, the patent literature is well covered in this publication. The Royal Society of Chemistry has entered the market with its monthly *Current Biotechnology Abstracts.* The contents are divided into four main sections: techniques, industrial areas, technocommercial, and information (books, journals, reviews). Each issue contains between 300 to 350 abstracts and is indexed by subject, chemical, and company. Finally, there is the *Telegen Reporter,* the all-embracing information package for the biotechnologist. It includes an abstracting service (direct from source material), sections on market highlights, corporate monitor, and events and meetings. Patents and book reports are also dealt with and there is an excellent index.

Journals from neighboring disciplines account for a major portion of the literature published in the field. Even just a cursory look at a bibliography on recombinant DNA technology will reveal the multidisciplinary publishing habits of the investigators working in the field. Major biochemistry journals such as *Journal of Biological Chemistry, Biochemistry, Biochemical Journal, FEBS Letters, Biochimica et Biophysica Acta,* and *Federation Proceedings* also cover molecular genetics material. *Journal of Molecular Biology, Cell, EMBO Journal, Journal of General Microbiology, Journal of Immunology, Journal of Bacteriology, Journal of Virology, Journal of Cell Biology,* and *Chromosoma* comprise a majority of the genetic engineering literature. Well known multi-science journals like *Nature, Science, Proceedings of the National Academy of Sciences,* and *Experientia* have a history of publishing important papers.

REVIEWS OF THE LITERATURE

Given the overwhelming task of staying current with the literature, a researcher often will need a state of the art survey of a subject. At such times the value of a good review article cannot be overestimated. There are two forms of review serial. The first is hard bound, and issuance is often annual. Well known examples of these include *Advances in Genetics, Advances in Human Genetics, Annual Review of Genetics,* and *Annual Review of Biochemistry.* The series *Advances in Biochemical Engineering/Biotechnology* published by Springer-Verlag, is the new title of the established series *Advances in Biochemical Engineering.* Volume 26 has two sections of interest to industrial microbiology. *Essays in Applied Microbiology* by J.R. Norris provides a perspective view rather than detailed examination of the latest research findings. This volume might be of more interest to industrial business managers who require knowledge of commercial processes but need not know all of the small details.

Published by Verlag Chemie International, a well-respected publisher of technical material for scientific research, the first three volumes of a comprehensive treatise have just been released. Entitled *Biotechnology,* this 8-volume series should be a welcome addition. It is aimed particularly at those involved in industrial microbiology and development and expansion of microbial processes.

There are two recent series titled *Genetic Engineering.* The first, begun in 1979 by Jane Setlow and Alexander Hollaender, is published by Plenum Press. The second is edited by Robert Williamson and is published by Academic Press. Both series are dedicated to reviewing important developments in the field and stress the rapidity of publication. The reviews in the Williamson series are on average about twice as long as those in the Setlow/Hollaender volume and, with one exception, are much more concerned with technical aspects, not with precise laboratory procedures. The volumes are no substitute for a collection of methods, like volumes 65 and 68 of *Methods in Enzymology,* but are good in that they concentrate on the planning of experimental protocols and the rationale behind alternative approaches. The Setlow/Hollaender volume covers a wide range of subject matter. The review articles are heterogeneous in style and purpose, and do not necessarily fulfill the promise of the subtitle of the series—"Principles and Methods."

The second type of review assumes the journal format—*CRC Critical Reviews in Biochemistry, CRC Critical Reviews in Microbiology,* and *CRC Critical Reviews in Biotechnology. Trends in Biochemistry* and *Trends in Biotechnology* combine the review aspect with news and information. They include short state of the art papers covering techniques and recent advances in biotechnology, as well as feature articles on funding, education, book reviews, and meeting announcements.

Convenient access to the prolific review literature is provided by the *Index of Biochemical Reviews,* published annually since 1971 as a supplement to FEBS Letters.

CONFERENCE PROCEEDINGS

As sources of information for scientists, formal meetings have a long and respectable history. Because many of the papers presented often report research work several months before publication in journals, conferences function as an early outlet in the dissemination process. Early findings in recombinant DNA technology were reported at the Gordon Conference on Nucleic Acids, held in New Hampshire in June 1973.[7] It is a policy of the Gordon Conferences that no abstracts or proceedings be published, but the work discussed at this particular Gordon was of such scientific and political import that it served as impetus to the first Asilomar Conference. The Asilomar Conferences are significant because they were the first formal meetings called expressly for the purpose of discussing potential risks of genetic engineering research. The first, held in January 1973, discussed the biohazards of work with animal viruses, and in particular, tumor viruses. The proceedings of the meeting were published by the Cold Spring Harbor Laboratories as a book titled *Biohazards in Biological Research.* The report from Asilomar II, held in February 1975, appeared in *Science* 188:991–994; 1975.

The Cold Spring Harbor Laboratories (CSH) sponsor and publish several conference series. Best known is the *Symposia on Quantitative Biology.* Published annually, each volume focuses on a particular aspect of molecular biology. Volume 43, for example, is "DNA—Replication and Recombination." The *Conferences on Cell Proliferation* have covered such topics as cell motility, tumor virology, and protein phosphorylation. The most recent series to come from CSH is the *Banbury Reports.* Over the past decade CSH has perceived an increased need for the advice of the geneticist in assessing public health consequences of environmental factors that may lead to increased risks of cancer, as well as many other diseases whose origins lie in changes in DNA. To help bring together the worlds of genetics and biological risk assessment the Banbury Center organizes these conferences of specialists from industry, regulatory agencies, academia, and governmental laboratories.

Other symposia which frequently deal with topics related to recombinant DNA include the *Brookhaven Symposia in Biology,* published by the Brookhaven National Laboratories, and from Academic Press, the *ICN—UCLA Symposia on Molecular and Cellular Biology,* and the *Miami Winter Symposia.*

PATENTS

The term "letters patent" or, more commonly, "patent," originally referred to an open letter or agreement conferring some right or privilege on the holder. Now used chiefly in reference to inventions, a patent is essentially a bargain struck between the state and the inventor. The state guarantees to the inventor the sole right for a certain period of years to make, use, or sell his inventions, in order that he may reap a fair reward for his efforts. History has shown that this stimulates capital investment in new manufacturing, and encourages growth of new industries. The potential profits from genetic engineering are exciting. New cell lines, new products made by cellular mini-factories, and new tools for genetic engineers have already been patented, and more will continue to be issued as companies race to develop microorganisms that can inexpensively produce vaccines and chemicals previously available only by costly methods. For more background on the subject of patents in the biosciences, the reader may want to refer to two books which have appeared recently. *Patenting Life Forms,* the proceedings of a Banbury Conference, discusses legal issues and includes comprehensive descriptions of American and European biotechnology patents issued and published to date. Intended as a practical guide for the research scientist involved in this industry, *Patenting in the Biological Sciences* may also be useful to those within companies and universities who must make business decisions with respect to research results in the biological sciences.

The task of tracking down genetic engineering patents can be overwhelming. These patents are dispersed into more than 150 classes and sub-classes in the U.S. Patent Office classification system. A recent publication titled *Genetic Engineering/Biotechnology Patents 1980/81* identifies all relevant patents issued by the U.S. Patent Office in 1980 and the first six months of 1981, and reproduces the full texts of these 40 "key patents." The Table of Contents lists patents by number, title, and assignee. Each month the journal *Biotechnology* lists recent patents with their abstracts. *Biotechnology Patent Digest* is a biweekly periodical providing information on patents in genetic engineering and related fields. Patents issued during the previous two weeks are listed, as well as news of forthcoming conferences, new publications, etc. For rapid retrospective and current awareness searching of the patent literature several online databases are available.[8] DIALOG offers the CLAIMS patent files, which is produced by IFI/Plenum Data Company, and provides access to over 1.3 million U.S. patents issued by the U.S. Patent and Trademark Office since 1950. BRS/PATDATA covers U.S. Patents since 1971, and is updated weekly, making it very current. The Derwent Patent files, available from SDC, offer the most comprehensive access, covering European as well as U.S. patents. Abstracts are included for most documents, and the unit record of U.S. patents includes full-text online access to claims data. Hard copies of patents can be ordered online both through DIALOG and ORBIT. Several commercial and non-profit suppliers of patents exist. Cost and speed of service are factors to be considered in evaluating the various sources.[9]

REGULATIONS AND COMPLIANCES

Any technology with such visibility and potential impact as recombinant DNA research has its attendant legal ramifications. Molecular biologists have been propelled, ready or not, into the circles of business and law, especially as they relate to federal agency regulations of the technology itself.[10]

Federal regulation of biotechnology has so far been confined to the *NIH Guidelines for Research Involving Recombinant DNA Molecules*. The Guidelines have been relaxed considerably since they were first formulated in 1976. Revisions and actions to the Guidelines are reported in the *Federal Register* (most recently in volume 48 (106): 24556-24581; 1983 June 1) as well as in the *Recombinant DNA Technical Bulletin*. The latter also has a section which deals with the analysis of legislation affecting genetic engineering, and articles on public policy, law and ethics. *The Congressional Record, Science and Government Report,* and *"The Blue Sheet"* are other timely sources of federal information.

ABSTRACTS AND INDEXES

Due to the multi-disciplinary nature of genetic engineering, the most reliable access to the literature still remains the four major indexes—*Biological Abstracts* (BA), *Chemical Abstracts* (CAS), *Index Medicus,* and *Science Citation Index* (SCI). *Biological Abstracts,* and its companion *BA/RRM,* have extensive coverage of not only the periodical literature, but also reviews, research reports, meetings and books in biology and biomedicine. The indexes provide five modes of access to the literature: 1. Author/Corporate; 2. Biosystematic indexes for broad taxonomic categories; 3. Generic index of organism names listed alphabetically at the genus-species level; 4. Concept index of broad subject headings of biological interest; 5. Subject index which utilizes the Keyword-in-Context format.

Chemical Abstracts is published weekly, arranged by subject groups, and each entry gives full bibliographic information and an abstract. Each issue has indexes by subject, author, and patent number, and these same indexes are cumulated twice a year, for January to June and for July to December. In searching the patent literature, however, the user is advised not to rely totally on the use of *Chemical Abstracts*, but to prefer the sources mentioned earlier. Of the 40 "key patents" identified by *Genetic Engineering/Biotechnology Patents 1980/81*, 25 were omitted by CAS. For example, *Chemical Abstracts* indexes U.S. Patent No. 4262090 for interferon production, but does not include U.S. No. 4273875 which covers plasmid pUC6 and the processing of the same. The Index Guide should be consulted for potential subject access to the General Subject Index. Among the headings available are "recombination, genetic," "molecular cloning," and "genetic engineering."

Probably the best known index in the field of biomedicine is *Index Medicus*. MeSH (Medical Subject Headings) is the controlled vocabulary that is used to index articles for MEDLARS, and is published annually as Part 2 of the January *Index Medicus*. MeSH is divided into two sections, the Annotated Alphabetic List and a hierarchical arrangement, called tree structures, sub-divided into 15 major categories. Each index term has an assigned number within the hierarchy:

Recombination, genetics	G5.832
DNA	D13.444.308
Genetic technics	E5.393.

During the indexing process the most specific terms available from MeSH are assigned to the document. Thus, if an article were concerned with "Genetic Intervention," it would be indexed under that subject heading rather than the broader "Genetics Technics."

Science Citation Index, well known for its unique Source/Citation/Permuterm indexing format, also provides information on industrial trends via its Corporate Index. For example, if you want to know what kind of work has been done at Genentech, the Corporate Index will direct you to the Geographic Index listing for California—San Francisco. The names of the primary authors are under the Genentech heading. Institute for Scientific Information's publications are notable also because they have been shown to be more current than their counterparts. The average time lag between the publication of an article in a journal and its appearance in *Science Citation Index* is 110 days, and only 31 days for weekly *Current Contents Life Sciences*.[11]

Additional coverage of genetics material can be found in *Excerpta Medica, Section 22: Human Genetics, IRL Life Sciences Collection,* and *Engineering Index.*

ONLINE SERVICES

The widespread availability of online bibliographic retrieval provides access to a variety of indexes, so it is not surprising that multi-database searching is the name of the game today. Many databases have unique features, both in terms of searchable elements and subject coverage. Table 2 summarizes the searchable fields of ten files which are potential sources of biotechnology/genetic engineering information.

Of course, duplication of coverage is unavoidable. An investigation of the journals abstracted by BA, CAS, and Engineering Index found that 27% of the 14,592 journals monitored were abstracted by two of the three services. Overlap between BA and CAS was 40%, and between Engineering Index and CAS was 43%.[12]

To compare the coverage of seven databases—BIOSIS, CAS, EXCERPTA MEDICA, LIFE SCIENCES, MEDLINE, SCISEARCH, TELEGEN—a search was performed on the molecular cloning of the *bacillus subtilis*. The results are summarized in Table 3.

Of the 56 references retrieved by the search, one was a book, three were patents, thirteen were conference papers, and thirty-nine were journal articles. There was no duplication of the patent, conference, or book data. The amount of overlap of the journal articles is shown below:

—11 articles were retrieved by 1 database
—6 articles were retrieved by 2 databases
—6 articles were retrieved by 3 databases
—5 articles were retrieved by 4 databases
—7 articles were retrieved by 5 databases
—3 articles were retrieved by 6 databases
—1 article was retrieved by all 7 databases.

TABLE 2: A Comparison of Searchable Fields in Biomedical Databases*

	BIOSIS	CAS	CLAIMS	COMP	CONF	EXMED	IRL	MEDLINE	SCI	TELEGEN
Abstracts online	X					X	X	X		X
Authors	X	X	X	X	X	X	X	X	X	X
Broad search codes	X	X	X	X	X	X	X	X		
Cited references									X	
Conference location					X					
Controlled vocabulary		X		X	X	X	X	X		X
Corporate Source/Author affiliation	X	X		X	X	X	X	X	X	X
Document type	X	X					X	X	X	X
Free text	X	X	X	X		X	X	X	X	X
Journal CODEN	X	X		X				X		
Journal title	X	X	X			X	X	X	X	X
Language	X	X				X	X	X	X	
Manufacturer's name			X			X				
Patents		X	X				X			X
Publisher		X				X	X			
Registry numbers (CAS)		X	X					X		
Restrict to major concepts	X			X		X		X		X
Year of publication	X	X				X	X	X	X	

* BIOSIS Previews   CLAIMS Patents   Conference Papers Index   IRL Life Sciences   Scisearch (SCI)
  Chemical Abstracts (CAS) Compendex   Excerpta Medica   MEDLINE (NLM)   Telegen

TABLE 3: Coverage of Biology Databases by Document Type

	BOOKS	CONFERENCES	JOURNALS	PATENTS
BIOSIS	1	8	14	0
CAS	0	0	20	3
EXCERPTA MEDICA	0	0	22	0
LIFE SCIENCES	0	0	18	0
MEDLINE	0	0	25	0
SCISEARCH	0	0	15	0
TELEGEN	0	5	8	0

It is interesting to note that although all seven services claim inclusion of conference material, only BIOSIS and TELEGEN retrieved these citations. Similarly, TELEGEN missed the patents that CAS picked up. This illustrates the need for the information specialist to become familiar with the content of the various online products, and to not rely solely on the publisher's description of the file.

CONCLUSION

Important useful advances have already occurred employing the techniques of recombinant DNA. Synthetic human insulin was marketed in September 1982. Antibodies produced by hybridomas have been approved for diagnostic use and prospects are excellent that viral diseases soon will be conquered by use of interferon or vaccine. As a result of the new technology, substantial improvements in human and animal health will occur in the next few years. Applied biology is now in a period of especially rapid progress, and rapid information flow is a key ingredient of its success.

REFERENCES

1. *McGraw-Hill encyclopedia of science and technology.* 5th ed. Vol. 6: 149; 1982.
2. Emery, Alan E.H. Recombinant DNA technology. *Lancet.*2:1406-1409; 1981 Dec. 19/26.
3. Cohen, Stanley N. The manipulation of genes. *Scientific American.* 233(1): 24-33; 1975 June.

4. Anderson, W. French; Diacumakos, Elaine G. Genetic engineering in mammalian cells. *Scientific American.* 245(1):106-121; 1981 July.

5. Alberts, Bruce (and others). *Molecular biology of the cell.* New York: Garland Publishing; 1983: p. 185, Table 4-12. 1146 p.

6. Davis, Julien. What's news in biotechnology? *Nature.* 229:493-496; 1982 Oct. 7.

7. Watson, J.D.; Tooze, John. *The DNA story.* San Francisco: W.H. Freeman; 1982: Chapter 1.

8. Kaback, Stuart M. Retrieving patent information online. *Online.* 2(1): 16-25; 1978 January.

9. Hunt, Dixie L. Sources of patent copies. *Science & Technology Libraries.* 2(4): 69-78; 1982 Summer.

10. Korwek, Edward L. Recombinant DNA and the law: review of some general legal considerations. *Gene.* 15: 1-5; 1981 July.

11. Poyer, Robert K. Time lag in four indexing services. *Special Libraries.* 73:142-146; 1982 April.

12. Wood, J.D. Overlap in the list of journals monitored by BIOSIS, CAS, and Ei. *Journal of the American Society for Information Science.* 23: 36-38; 1972.

APPENDIX 1
JOURNALS AND SERIES DISCUSSED

Abstracts of Biocommerce
Advances in Biochemical Engineering/Biotechnology
Advances in Genetics
Advances in Human Genetics
Annual Review of Biochemistry
Annual Review of Genetics
Applied Genetics News
Blue Sheet
Biochimica et Biophysica Acta
Biochemical Genetics
Biochemical Journal
Biochemistry
Bioengineering News
Bioscience
Biotechnology
Biotechnology Law Report
Biotechnology News
Biotechnology Patent Digest
Brookhaven Symposia in Biology
Cell
Chromosoma
Cold Spring Harbor Conferences on Cell Proliferation
Cold Spring Harbor Symposia on Quantitation Biology
Congressional Record
CRC Critical Reviews in Biochemistry
CRC Critical Reviews in Biotechnology
CRC Critical Reviews in Microbiology
Current Biotechnology Abstracts
Derwent Biotechnology Abstracts

DNA: A Journal of Molecular Biology
DNA Repair Reports
EMBO Journal
Essays in Applied Microbiology
Experientia
FEBS Letters
Federation Proceedings
Federal Register
Gene
Genetical Research
Genetic Engineering News
Genetics
Human Genetics
ICN-UCLA Symposia on Molecular and Cellular Biology
Journal of Bacteriology
Journal of Cell Biology
Journal of Molecular and Applied Genetics
Journal of Molecular Biology
Journal of Biological Chemistry
Journal of General Microbiology
Journal of Immunology
Journal of Virology
Methods in Enzymology
Miami Winter Symposia
Molecular and General Genetics
Mutation Research
Nature
Plasmids
Proceedings of the National Academy of Sciences
Quarterly Reviews of Biology
Recombinant DNA Technical Bulletin
Scientific American
Science and Government Report
Science
Telegen Reporter
Trends in Biochemistry
Trends in Biotechnology

APPENDIX 2
MONOGRAPHS DISCUSSED

Alberts, Bruce (and others). *Molecular biology of the cell.* New York: Garland Publishing; 1983.
Biotechnology made simple: a glossary of recombinant DNA and hybridoma technology. Richmond, U.K.: PFB Publications; 1983.
Crespi, R.S. *Patenting in the biological sciences.* New York: John Wiley; 1982.
Davis, R.W. *Advanced bacterial genetics.* New York: Cold Spring Harbor; 1980.
Dwyer, Paula E. *Genetic engineering/biotechnology patents 1980/81.* Wash. D.C.: McGraw-Hill; 1982.

Fasman, Gerald D. *CRC handbook of biochemistry and molecular biology*, 3d ed. Boca Raton, FL: CRC Press; 1976.
Friedberg, Errol C.; Hanawalt, Philip C. *DNA repair: a laboratory manual of research procedures.* New York: Marcel Dekker; 1981, 1983.
Glover, D.M. *Genetic engineering: cloning DNA.* New York: Chapman and Hall; 1980.
Hellman, H. (and others). *Biohazards in biological research.* New York: Cold Spring Harbor; 1973.
Judson, H.F. *The eighth day of creation.* New York: Simon and Schuster; 1979.
Kohler, George. *Hybridoma techniques.* New York: Cold Spring Harbor; 1980.
Kornberg, Arthur. *DNA replication.* San Francisco: W.H. Freeman; 1980.
Kornberg, Arthur. *DNA replication, 1982 supplement.* San Francisco: W.H. Freeman; 1982.
Laskan, Allen I.; Lechevalier, H. *CRC handbook of microbiology,* 2d ed. Boca Raton, FL: CRC Press; 1977-1982.
Lehninger, Albert. *Biochemistry: the molecular basis of all structure and function.* New York: Worth; 1975.
Maniatis, T. *Molecular cloning: a laboratory manual.* New York: Cold Spring Harbor; 1983.
Menditto, Joseph; Kirsch, Debbie. *Genetic engineering, DNA, and cloning: a bibliography in the future of genetics.* Troy, N.Y.: Whitston; 1983.
Miller, Jeffrey. *Experiments in molecular genetics.* New York: Cold Spring Harbor; 1972.
Pergolizzi, Robert G. *Genetic engineering/biotechnology sourcebook.* Wash. D.C.: McGraw-Hill, 1982.
Plant, David W. (and others). *Patenting of life forms.* New York: Cold Spring Harbor; 1983.
Rehm, H.J.; Reed, G. *Biotechnology: a comprehensive treatise.* Deerfield Beach, FL: Verlag Chemie International; 1982, 1983.
Schlief, R.F.; Wensink, P.C. *Practical methods in molecular biology.* New York: Springer Verlag; 1981.
Setlow, Jane K.; Hollaender, Alexander. *Genetic engineering: principles and methods:* New York: Plenum Press; 1979-1982. v. 1-4.
Stryer, Lubert. *Biochemistry.* 2d ed. San Francisco: W.H. Freeman; 1981.
Walton, Alan G.; Hammer, Sharon K. *Genetic engineering and biotechnology yearbook 1983.* Amsterdam: Elsevier; 1983.
Watson, James D.; Tooze, J. *The DNA story: a documentary history of gene cloning.* San Francisco: W.H. Freeman; 1982.
Watson, James D. *Molecular biology of the gene.* 3d ed. Menlo Park, CA: Benjamin/Cummings; 1976.
Weir, B.S. *Statistical analysis of DNA sequence data.* New York: Marcel Dekker; 1983.
Williamson, R. *Genetic engineering.* New York: Academic Press; 1979, 1982. v. 1-3.
Work, T.S.; Work, E. *Laboratory techniques in biochemistry and molecular biology.* Amsterdam: Elsevier; 1975-83. v. 1-11.

SPECIAL PAPER

Science and Technology Academic Facility Construction in Louisiana-Oklahoma-Texas, 1977-1982

Frank L. Turner
Bernard S. Schlessinger
Kristin Sandefur

ABSTRACT. Study of 17 academic library constructions, in the period 1977-1982, in Texas, Louisiana and Oklahoma, reveals that these Sunbelt states have been generous in their support of academic library construction. Major findings are that 1) almost all construction was of a general nature; 2) the major issue precipitating construction was space; 3) construction dollars, square footage and seating were all directly correlated with size, type, and complexity of institutions; 4) the new libraries exhibited a surprisingly traditional posture in many respects.

INTRODUCTION

The Sunbelt states generally, and the three states of Texas, Oklahoma, and Louisiana in particular, have in the last five years experienced a remarkable influx of new residents eager to take ad-

---

Frank L. Turner (BA, MA, MSLS, PhD) is Professor of Library Science at Texas Woman's University, Denton, TX 76204. Bernard S. Schlessinger (BS, MS, MLS, PhD) is Professor of Library Science and Associate Dean at Texas Woman's University, Denton, TX 76204. Kristin Sandefur (BFA) is a MLS candidate at Texas Woman's University, Denton, TX 76204.

© 1984 by The Haworth Press, Inc. All rights reserved.

vantage of the newer information-based industries as well as a resurgent emphasis on petrochemicals. While much of the United States has been in economic recession, Texas, Oklahoma, and Louisiana have enjoyed a prosperity envied by all. Although a five-year period (since July 1977) is a rather short range upon which to base definitive conclusions about the effects of this phenomenon upon academic library construction (and, in particular, library facilities for science and technology), it is instructive to make some comparisons based upon the statistics which have over the years been published in *Library Journal*.[1]

A comparison of the number of academic library construction projects (i.e., new libraries, additions, and additions and renovations) in the three states under study, with the United States and Canada as a whole is outlined in Table 1.

A comparison of money spent on new academic libraries, additions, and additions and renovations is shown in Table 2.

Based on these statistics, which clearly do not reveal the extent of pre-1978 construction nor hint at projects now in the planning stage, it would seem that the three states, taken as a whole, in the five-year period have been duly spreading their bounty upon academic library facilities, averaging 9.2% of the total expenditure spent on academic library facilities in the United States and Canada. Of particular note are projects such as the following: new libraries at Texas Tech University, Pan American University, Trinity University, University of Texas at El Paso (Physical Sciences), University of Texas at Austin (Chemistry), Southwestern Baptist Theological Seminary, and the University of Oklahoma; and significant additions/renovations at Northeast Louisiana State University, Texas A & M University, University of Southwestern Louisiana, University of Tulsa, and St.

	Number of projects in TX, OK, LA	Number of projects in U.S. and Canada
1978-79	8	66
1980	3	27
1981	1	30
1982	3	35
Totals	15	158

TABLE 1. A comparison of the number of academic library construction projects.

	Dollars spent in TX, OK, LA	Dollars spent in U.S. & Canada	% of total dollars spent by 3 states
1978-79	31.6 mil	317.6 mil	10%
1980	17.4 mil	122.2 mil	14%
1981	5.6 mil	139.9 mil	4%
1982	15.6 mil	173.7 mil	9%

TABLE 2. A comparison of money spent on new academic libraries, additions, and additions and renovations.

Edward's University. This study was undertaken to find out more about these projects and their impact on science and technology resources.

METHODOLOGY

The data on which this discussion is based were derived from an interview/questionnaire format, which was mailed approximately two weeks before a telephone interview to academic library directors who had been identified in the pre-search through issues of *Library Journal.* The directors were asked to answer those questions which they could answer, and to await a telephone interview, at which time they might ask questions and complete the forms.

The 16 questions asked in the interview/questionnaire format identified the library and librarian; established whether the construction was of a total library or an expansion; a) of which science and technology was only a part, or b) which specifically served one discipline or several disciplines in science and technology; determined whether an outside consultant had been used; probed years, cost and other details of construction; asked for the square footage of the new construction and the approximate percentage devoted to science and technology and to various functions; covered the types of users, and special provisions for special groups and special services; and established the form of the general catalog and its searching, and the nature of the shelving and the collection. In addition, the directors were asked for a drawing of the layout and a glossy photo of the facility.

In all, 17 libraries were included in the final tabulation—13 in Texas, 2 in Louisiana, 2 in Oklahoma. Four of the libraries were in two-year institutions, 5 were in smaller four-year liberal arts-oriented institutions, 8 were in multi-purpose university settings.

DATA FROM QUESTIONNAIRES

The data from the questionnaires resulted in the following tabulations:

— Almost all the construction (15 of 17 facilities) in the Southwest was of a general nature. The era of building special-purpose libraries for science and technology seems to be ended, although two such units had been built at campuses of the University of Texas system. The practice of using consultants also seems to be less prevalent than before, with planning placed in the hands of the architects alone in 13 of the institutions.
— Construction dollars were directly correlated to size of institution, and to the complexity of offerings/degrees.
— Although university dollars were the major source of funding (an average of 73%, and better than 50% in 9 cases), donors were a major source as well (noted in 7 instances and averaging 54% in those). Federal dollars were, for the most part, a small factor.
— The major issue that precipitated construction was space—both stack and seating.
— Some interesting statistics:

* Average square footage added was 93,275, with a range from 11,000 to 375,000, and a total of 1,492,400. There was a direct correlation with type of library.
* Average cost of added space was 4.8 million dollars, with a range from one million to 13.1 million, and a total of 52.9 million.
* For the 10 schools that reported figures for the percentage of new construction devoted to science and technology, the average figure was 25%. The two-year institution average was around 15%, the four-year institution average 33%, and the multi-purpose university average 26%. Although the sample size is small and therefore, perhaps, not representative, it is not unexpected to find science and technology occupying a greater share of the space in larger institutions. The decrease in space occupied for the multi-purpose universities might be

anticipated if one assumes a certain degree of saturation of the science interest at the four-year level, with the volume of research materials in the humanities and social sciences increasing more rapidly in the post-graduate-oriented sections of the multi-purpose institutions.

* Public services and collection services together occupied about 80% of space added, technical services about 15%, administrative services about 5%.
* 12,250 seats were added in the 16 institutions responding, with averages of 160 seats for two-year colleges, 860 for four-year, 1040 for multi-purpose. Smaller institutions generally favored more traditional seating, with two-year institutions reporting 70% of such seating, and four-year and multi-purpose universities averaging 48%. This is notable, since two-year institutions generally pride themselves on their nontraditional approaches.

— Although 13 of the 17 libraries indicated that they had planned the facilities with the handicapped in mind, and 11 had given special consideration to microform service, the new libraries exhibited a traditional posture when one considers that:

* Only 6 of the 17 had included in their planning provisions for bibliographic instruction.
* Only 7 of the 17 had considered the implications of online services in their planning.
* Fourteen of the 17 have their general catalog in card form, with only two in fiche form, only one in computerized form.
* Only 3 libraries make available an OCLC terminal for public use, only one a catalog/searching terminal.
* Almost all had only fixed traditional shelving.
* The vast percentage of holdings (80%) seem still to be bound materials.

It would be hoped that, in the future, a greater percentage of new libraries would worry about bibliographic instruction, online services, and other newer developments in planning facilities.

One must remember that this study was of new construction in three states over a five-year period when major changes were taking place in academic library service patterns. It would be interesting to see if the same results were true in other parts of the country and whether any new trends will emerge in the next five years.

SCIENCE-TECHNOLOGY FACILITIES

As noted above, two facilities were built in the period that were totally devoted to science-technology facilities. These are reviewed below, in recognition of the possible interest on the part of the reader.

1. The John W. Mallet Chemistry Library on the Austin campus of the University of Texas, completed in 1978, serves the teaching and research activities of the Departments of Chemistry, Chemical Engineering and Nutrition. Financed by a combination of university and federal funding, its 11,400 square feet replaced a previous facility with 3200 square feet, which had been judged lacking in space, security, and compatibility with new technology. Statistically, the new facility:

— has a collection which includes approximately 21,000 bound monographs, 21,000 bound serials, and 900 microforms.
— devotes its space 25% to public services and 75% to collection services, these percentages including minimal space devoted to technical and administrative services.
— contains 117 seats distributed between carrels and tables, with 50% on perimeter walls.
— serves approximately 1200 undergraduates, 400 graduates, and 60+ faculty.
— maintains a card catalog.
— uses fixed-location traditional shelving.

2. The Physical Sciences Library on the El Paso campus of the University of Texas, completed in 1978, includes collections devoted to Science, Engineering, Mathematics, and Government Documents. Financed completely by university/state funds, the 1.5 million dollars facility's 25,000 square feet replaced previous space of 2,500 square feet, because of deterioration of that space and lack of seating and stack space. Statistically, the new facility:

— has a collection distributed 40% to bound monographs, 45% to bound serials, 15% to microforms.
— devotes its space 40% to public services and 60% to collection services, these percentages including minimal space devoted to technical and administrative services.

—contains 200+ seats, distributed 80% in carrels, 20% at tables, with no seating on perimeter walls.
—serves approximately 14,500 undergraduates, 1,000 graduates, and 450 faculty.
—maintains a card catalog.
—makes special provisions for the handicapped, bibliographic instruction and microforms.
—uses fixed-location traditional shelving.

REFERENCE

1. *Library Journal,* Dec. 1, 1979; Dec. 1, 1980; Dec. 1, 1981; Dec. 1, 1982.

NEW REFERENCE WORKS IN SCIENCE AND TECHNOLOGY

Robert G. Krupp, Editor

Reviewers for this issue are: Kathy L. Belyea (KLB), Technical Library, Bell Laboratories, Whippany, NJ; Carmela Carbone (CC), Engineering Societies Library, New York, NY; Robert G. Krupp (RGK), Maplewood, NJ; and Barbara Walcott (BW), Health Sciences Library, Columbia University, New York, NY.

EARTH SCIENCES

Assessment of manganese nodule resources: the data and methodologies. (Seabed Minerals Series; vol. 1). London: Graham and Trotman, in cooperation with the United Nations; 1982. 79p. $26.00. ISBN 0-86010-347-1.

> This is the beginning of a nine-volume series dealing with minerals in the seabed, all concerned specifically with manganese nodules. Despite the slimness of the work, it provides a concise and thorough discussion of how much of these resources (manganese nodules) exist in the ocean. The quality and quantity of data collected to date are examined and available estimates are reviewed. Not only for geologists and chemists but also for a much broader audience including lawyers, public entrepreneurs, and investors. (RGK)

Crowson, Phillip. *Minerals handbook, 1982–83.* New York: Van Nostrand; 1982. $25.00. ISBN 0-442-21504-5.

> This introductory guide covers the international supply and demand characteristics of thirty-seven minerals and metals. Spe-

cial coverage is given to gems and minerals of Europe, Japan, the United Kingdom, and the United States. The work is arranged in two parts with the first containing eight tables which summarize the data contained in the second part, i.e., the detailed tables of the thirty-seven minerals. For each mineral, reserve statistics (albeit from 1980/81) are presented first and grouped by developed, less developed, and centrally planned nations. Additional data for each mineral includes world reserves and production, adequacy, consumption, value, prices, marketing and trade statistics. Most of the data is cited for the period 1976–1981, especially in regard to pricing. Although the work is primarily for the non-specialist, it is a must for any geology and gemnology library, and especially where economic analysts hold forth. Nevertheless it is not a substitute for the many prime source publications listed in the Appendix. (KLB)

LIFE SCIENCES

Birrer, Richard B.; Birrer, Christina D. *Medical diagnostic signs; a reference collection of eponymic bedside signs.* Springfield, IL: C. C. Thomas. 108p. $24.75. ISBN 0-398-04541-0.

This is an alphabetical listing of eponymic diagnostic signs. Each entry provides, where available, the full name, dates, nationality, and specialty of the physician who first described the sign. A concise definition of the sign is given, followed by the reference to the article or book in which the sign was originally described. In most cases, an additional reference is provided to a source of biographical information on the physician. Synonyms and cross references are also included. The feature of this little book that will earn it a place on many medical reference shelves is that the authors succeeded in tracking down references to the literature for so many of these signs. (BW)

Health science books 1876–1982. New York: Bowker; 1982. 4 v. $200.00. ISBN 0-8352-1447-8.

This four-volume work is a bibliography of over 132,000 books that have been published in the United States since 1876 and cataloged by the Library of Congress. Subject coverage is broad, including the basic biomedical sciences, allied health, and related fields. The entries, selected from the *American Book Publishing Record* database, are arranged by Library of Congress subject headings in the first three volumes. Each full entry provides cataloging information prepared by the Library of Congress and presented in a clear format that looks like a compressed catalog card. Cross references guide users from National Library of Medicine *Medical Subject Headings* (MeSH) to the appropriate Library of Congress (LC) subject headings. The fourth volume consists of an author index, a title index, and two subject headings guides. These guides list MeSH headings and their approximate LC equivalents, and vice-versa.

As in any work of this scope, errors can be found. For instance, a small section of books on ships slipped past the editors. Overall, though, the breadth of coverage makes this an invaluable resource. In health science libraries of all sizes it will be used for verifications and for its retrospective subject bibliographies; in small libraries it will serve as an inexpensive source of cataloging information as well. (BW)

McInnis, Raymond G. *Research guide for psychology.* Westport, CT: Greenwood Press; 1982. 604p. $45.00. ISBN 0-313-21399-2.

The purpose of this guide, according to its author, is to assist investigators in identifying those information sources, among the many that are available, that will be useful in their research. To accomplish this, almost 1,200 bibliographic and "substantive" information sources are discussed. After the first chapter, which covers general works, the material is organized by broad subject headings adapted from the classification scheme used by *Psychological Abstracts.* Within each subject section, sources are arranged by type: research guides, substantive information sources, substantive-bibliographic sources, and bibliographic information sources. Each section is designed to be informative by itself, but a letter-and-number code is used to refer the reader to the first discussion of a given source. Most titles are described in detail, and, for some, critical reviews from the journal literature are cited. All sources covered are listed by code in a bibliography near the end of the book, and an author, title, and subject index is provided. The availability of some sources in machine-readable form is not mentioned consistently, and the classification scheme used is a bit confusing at first. Nevertheless, this guide is very readable and comprehensive, and should prove most useful in directing researchers and reference or bibliographic instruction librarians beyond the familiar sources. (BW)

PHYSICAL SCIENCES

Cheremisinoff, Nicholas P.; Gupta, R., eds. *Handbook of fluids in motion*. Ann Arbor: Ann Arbor Science; 1983. 1,202p. $79.95. ISBN 0-250-40458-3.

This handbook-*cum*-encyclopedia is a truly weighty reference work covering applied fluid mechanics. Considerable emphasis is given modelling approaches in relation to the physics controlling flow phenomenon. The chapter references and readings are exceptionally up-to-date. For a broad spectrum of engineering research collections. (RGK)

Parker, S. P., ed. *McGraw-Hill encyclopedia of chemistry*. New York: McGraw-Hill; 1982. 1,195p. $49.50. ISBN 0-07-045484-1.

This is a comprehensive reference tool dealing with the major divisions of theoretical chemistry and also includes relevant topics on physics. The almost 800 articles, arranged alphabetically from "Absorption" to "Zirconium," were selected from the *McGraw-Hill encyclopedia of science and technology* (5th edition, 1982). Hundreds of items of illustrative matter supplement the text. The index is well-developed. For undergraduate libraries on chemistry and public libraries not owning the full encyclopedia. (RGK)

Parker, S. P., ed. *McGraw-Hill encyclopedia of physics.* New York: McGraw-Hill; 1983. 1,343p. $54.50. ISBN 0-07-045253-9.

This is a rather comprehensive and fairly up-to-date alphabetic arrangement of 760 articles selected from the authoritative *McGraw-Hill encyclopedia of science and technology* (5th edition, 1982). Coverage is from "Aberration (optics)" through "Zeeman effect" reflecting not only basic principles but also recent advances as well, plus selected topics in mathematics. Over 1,000 drawings, graphs, charts, and photographs supplement the text. The index is quite thorough. For academic and larger public libraries, particularly if the full encyclopedia is not available. (RGK)

TECHNOLOGY

Arnould, Michael; Zubibi, Fabio, eds. *English-French petroleum dictionary.* Paris: Dunod; 1981. 267p. $37.00. ISBN 2-04-011414-9.

Over 8,700 terms on petroleum technology are translated from English to French and arranged alphabetically in this truly useful dictionary, primarily for special libraries and as personal copies for translators. The preface and introduction are in French. A lengthy list of publications consulted during preparation of the work is included. (RGK)

Belding, William G., ed. *ASM Handbook of engineering mathematics.* Metals Park, Ohio: American Society for Metals; 1983. 697 p. $72.00. ISBN 0-87170-157-X.

This handbook is intended to serve as a practical reference tool for engineers and for engineering students with basic background in college-level mathematics. In each area of basic mathematics, key equations are presented without detailed derivations. The branches of mathematics emphasized are those useful in the design and manufacturing environment of the typical metalworking company. Part I of the handbook contains basic equations and theorems of algebra, trigonometry, geometry, analytical geometry, calculus, etc., in ascending order of difficulty. In Part II, mathematical equations and illustrations present key elements of various disciplines of mechanical engineering. The focus is on those equations that help lead to solutions of practical problems in mechanical analysis and design. Lists of selected references are provided at the end of each chapter in Part II. (CC)

British Kinomatograph Sound and Television Society. *Dictionary of audio-visual terms.* London: Focal Press; 1983. 138p. $24.95. ISBN 0-240-51201-4.

Compilers of this dictionary interpret "audio-visual" rather generously by embracing the preparation of pictures and sound by film and video as well as by tape-slide, film-strip, and multivision. Some 2,000 terms (many with accompanying illustrative matter) are included. A few of the definitions are wordy, but most run less than 20 words. Thirteen appendices cover topics such as image areas, seating layouts for viewing, plus other technical-oriented diagrams and tables. For special libraries in the field. (RGK)

Churchwell, Jan W.; Chaudier, Louanna, eds. *Who's who in technology today.* 3d ed. Highland Park, Ill.: J. Dick; 1982. 4 volumes. $385/set. ISBN 0-943692-00-8 (for complete set).

This is a four-volume data base of biographical information of scientists and engineers contributing to technological growth. Volume 1 involves electronic and physics technologies; volume 2 mechanical, civil, and earth science technologies; and volume 3 chemical and bioscience technologies. Included are 27,000 capsuled biographies, patents, expertise, leadership, and honors. Unfortunately, no dates are associated with an individual's indicated current affiliation. Thus one is likely to assume *that* affiliation begins immediately after the last year of the immediate previous position, and that it is still extant. Such an assumption may be incorrect. Volume 4 provides two indexes (as its only contributions): some 80,000 principal expertise listings and the index of names for the first three volumes of the set, although each of these volumes has its own index of names. Verily, this is another expensive reference tool, but it should be considered by any science and technology library requiring yet one more in the growing array of technical subject who's-who volumes to lessen the chances of near-misses in questions of biographical data. (RGK)

Harvey, Philip D., ed. *Engineering properties of steel.* Metals Park, Ohio: American Society for Metals; 1982. 527 p. ISBN 0-87170-144-8. (Price not available.)

Materials selected for industrial applications are usually a compromise of properties, costs, availability, and suitability. Hence, engineers must frequently survey a large number of steels for a particular application. This handbook provides the information to make such surveys quickly and efficiently. It presents the chemical composition, mechanical properties, general characteristics and uses, and machining data for most steels used in industrial applications. Data are given for carbon, alloy, stainless and heat resisting, tool, ASTM structural, and maraging steels. The data listed for each steel should be regarded as average or nominal and adjustments made to suit the prevailing conditions. Where applicable, data for the steels are arranged in numerical order according to the AISI/SAE identification number. The ASTM structural steels are given in numerical order using the ASTM standard specification number. Maraging steels are given in the order of nominal yield strength. For the AISI/SAE Steels, the designations of similar steels as listed by United States and foreign standards of specification organizations are given. There is a cross-reference list from the foreign or other U.S. designation to the AISI/SAE designation of the steel. (CC)

Hunt, V. Daniel. *Industrial robotics handbook.* New York: Industrial Press; 1983. 432 p. ISBN 0-8311-1148-8. (Price not available.)

This handbook is a comprehensive overview of industrial robots. It describes applications for robots, defines procedures for system selection and discusses relevant computer programming and integration details. It presents the technical characteristics of over 80 systems and describes the major industrial robots being sold in the United States. The impact of robots on workers and their jobs is discussed and experts' views on the future of industrial robots are presented. The book can serve as a reference source for the professional and for individuals interested in learning more about acquiring and using industrial robots for increasing productivity and reducing manufacturing costs. (CC)

Kaliske, Gisbert, comp. *Dictionary of plastics technology in four languages, English, German, French, Russian.* New York: Elsevier Science; 1982. 408p. $74.00. ISBN 0-444-99687-7.

This multilingual dictionary includes terms on materials, production aids, processing, and applications concerned with plastics technology. Basic science terms and those from related fields (e.g., coatings technology) are also contained in the listings. About 8,700 terms are arranged first in English with parallel columns of translations into German, French, and then Russian. Each entry is coded (e.g., "abhesion" is Al). Conversion from one of the non-English languages is accomplished through separate alphabetic sections which refer back to the main listing via the entry code (e.g., for "Abbau," see D25). For special libraries, translators, and strong technology collections containing foreign language works in plastics technology. (RGK)

Longly, Dennis; Shain, M., comps. *Dictionary of information technology.* New York: Wiley; 1982. 381p. $34.95. ISBN 0-471-89574-1.

In this work of some 6,500 terms used in the world of information technology, the subject is defined very broadly to involve virtually every aspect of communication and related hardware. Included too is jargon from fields such as printing and publishing, photography and cinematography, and word processing and business systems. One further feature is the inclusion of eleven essays on important topics such as microcomputers, programming, and computer networks. These are located within the body of the dictionary at the appropriate alphabetic points. For virtually all technology libraries in industry, academe, and larger public libraries. (RGK)

Parker, Sybil P., ed. *McGraw-Hill encyclopedia of engineering.* New York: McGraw-Hill Book Co.; 1983. 1264 p. $57.50. ISBN 0-07-045486-8.

This is an interdisciplinary work designed to provide information on ten major branches of engineering: civil, design, electrical industrial, mechanical, metallurgical, mining, nuclear, petroleum, and production engineering. The mechanical, electrical, and thermodynamical principles that are basic to all fields of engineering are also covered. The volume consists of more than 690 articles selected from the *McGraw-Hill encyclopedia of science and technology* (5th ed., 1982) covering topics from "acceleration" to "zone refining." Most entries provide bibliographies for further reading. The encyclopedia is intended for engineers, students, librarians, technical writers, and all others concerned with the theory and practice of engineering. (CC)

Traister, John E. *Handbook of power generation: transformers and generators.* Englewood Cliffs, N.J.: Prentice-Hall; 1983. 246p. $19.95. ISBN 0-13-380816-5.

This highly specialized reference tool dwells on theories (albeit only briefly) but more importantly (in depth) on the practical on-the-job aspects for a wide spectrum of applications in electrical power generation and distribution. The author details available equipment and then deftly shows by illustrations and examples how to use it. An excellent support for texts in electrical engineering. No author affiliation is given. (RGK)

Ziauddin, Sardor, ed. *Science and technology in the Middle East: a guide to issues, organizations, and institutions.* London: Longman; 1982. 324p. $85.00. ISBN 0-582-90052-2.

> This reference guide to the scientific and technological activity in the Middle East covers the region from Morocco on the west to Pakistan on the east, and from Turkey on the north to Sudan on the south, embracing in all some nineteen countries. (Israel will have its own separate coverage.) The first part is a critical description of scientific and technological developments in the region since 1975. Emphasis is placed on trends. However, there is a striking bibliography covering 1975–1981. Part II describes the origins and projects of five major regional science and technology organizations. The final section concerns (for each country) an account of the organization and administration of science and technology, and government and academic research institutions plus their research projects. The appendix contains a list (by country) of almost 200 major establishments with addresses. For industrial, government, and larger public libraries. (This is the first volume in a new series on science and technology activities in the world today.) (RGK)

EXTANT SERIES

Encyclopedia of chemical processing and design. Vol. 17. New York: Dekker; 1983. 468p. $115.00. ISBN 0-8247-2451-8 (v. 1).

> Coverage includes 23 alphabetically arranged topics from "Drying, Solids" through "Electrostatic Hazards: Basic Concepts." Not all contributions sport bibliographies and those which do contain very few citations after 1979. Of the 30 contributors, 22 have industrial affiliations. (RGK)

Fattorini, H. O. *The Cauchy problem.* (Encyclopedia of mathematics and its applications. Vol. 18.) Reading, Mass.: Addison-Wesley; 1983. 636p. $69.95. ISBN 0-201-13517-5.

> This volume, a continuation of a formidable series, is devoted to the "abstract Cauchy problem," a major perplexity of the theory of partial differential equations. Over 1,600 references are cited. For serious mathematics collections. (RGK)

Henderson, Faye and others, eds. *Information sources, 1983-84: the annual directory of the Information Industry Association.* 8th ed. Washington, D.C.: Information Industry Association; 1983. Member $21.00, Non-member $37.50. ISBN 0-942744-11-6.

> This is a continuation of a valuable guide suitable for general collections. All sections remain as heretofore although accurately updated. (KLB)

Kirk-Othmer encyclopedia of chemical technology. Vol. 21. 3d. ed. New York: Wiley; 1983. 968p. $180.00. ISBN 0-471-02074-5.

> Covers the topics "silver and silver alloys" through "sulfolanes and sulfones" in 34 recently documented essays. For example, the piece on "Space Chemistry" is a beautiful, compact (24 pages) presentation on a subject usually ascribed to astronomy but here shown in its proper slot within the framework of chemistry. (RGK)

Shafer, Wade H., ed. *Masters theses in the pure and applied sciences accepted by colleges and universities of the United States.* Vol. 26, New York: Plenum; 1982. 321p. $75.00. ISBN 0-306-41343-4.

> For the thesis year 1981, this volume presents a listing of 11,048 thesis titles from 218 United States and (despite the omission in the title) 24 Canadian universities. For academic libraries with masters degree programs in the sciences. (RGK)

SCI-TECH ONLINE

Ellen Nagle, Editor

DATABASE NEWS

Online Training Files

Two vendors recently announced databases which augment existing online training programs. These databases cover several key subject areas in science and technology, and also offer the opportunity for novice searchers to learn and utilize the basic search system commands.

The National Library of Medicine (NLM) has announced that an updated version of the *MEDLEARN* computer-aided instruction (CAI) program was made available in June 1983. While the content on basic MEDLINE and MeSH mechanics remains essentially the same, all program examples have been updated to reflect the 1983 MeSH Vocabulary and the current ELHILL software.

MEDLEARN first became available to the NLM online network in October 1976. Since that time, this CAI program has been used by thousands of individuals prior to their attendance at NLM's beginning training course. Completion of *MEDLEARN* prior to in-class instruction insures that all trainees have had at least a minimal exposure to the basic mechanics of online searching on the MEDLARS system and to the MEDLINE database. In addition, these trainees acquire experience logging in to NLM via the telecommunication networks of TELENET and TYMNET. *MEDLEARN* is also used extensively within organizations as a component of in-house backup searcher training programs.

Two MEDLINE simulated searches are included to provide the user of *MEDLEARN* with the opportunity to formulate and execute a search, have the strategy evaluated, and then perform the search in MEDLINE if so desired.

MEDLEARN will take the novice user a minimum of 3-4 hours to complete. It may be completed in one online session or in several segments, according to personal preference. All instructions on how to use *MEDLEARN* are contained in the *MEDLEARN* program. The only additional material required to complete the program is a copy of the *Medical Subject Headings (MeSH)*. It is recommended that *MEDLEARN* be used with a hardcopy terminal. Charges for *MEDLEARN* are $22 per connect hour in prime time; $15 per connect hour in non-prime time.

DIALOG has added two files to its ONTAP (ONline Training and Practice) series: *ONTAP BIOSIS Previews* and *ONTAP CAB Abstracts*. There are now 12 ONTAP files covering a wide variety of subjects, which can be used for self-instructional experimentation, to develop training materials, or to conduct formal workshops or classes on searching. They also afford an inexpensive opportunity for searchers to learn about databases with which they are unfamiliar. The price for searching any ONTAP files is $15 per connect time.

ONTAP BIOSIS Previews, available as File 205, consists of 24,000 BIOSIS records from the January 1980 update. The database is comprised of citations from Biological Abstracts and *Biological Abstracts/Reports, Reviews, Meetings.* All life sciences subjects are covered. Material includes periodical literature, monographs, books, technical reports, published theses, meetings, nomenclature rules, letters, annual reports, bibliographies and guides.

ONTAP CAB Abstracts (File 250) covers every branch of the agricultural sciences, including cooperatives, economics, education, engineering, genetics, pest control, rural planning, and taxonomy. It consists of records from *CAB Abstracts* for the first 3 months of 1980. The Commonwealth Agricultural Bureaux, publisher of the abstract journals, includes the following types of material in their database: scientific journals, books, monographic series, book reviews, technical reports, published theses, symposia, conference proceedings, review journals, patents, annual reports, bibliographies and guides, and translated journals. *ONTAP CAB Abstracts* contains approximately 36,000 records.

Full Text Chemical Journals Online

The American Chemical Society (ACS) and BRS jointly announced the availability of the *ACS Primary Journal Database.* The database offers full text coverage of more than 30,000 articles appearing in 18 primary chemistry journals published by the American Chemical Society from 1980 to the present. Print counterparts include: *Analytical Chemistry, Biochemistry, Journal of Organic Chemistry, Journal of Physical Chemistry, Journal of the American Chemical Society* and *Environmental Science and Technology.* Documents include complete title, authorship and imprint information in addition to the complete text of articles, footnotes, references, and captions. The file is updated biweekly to maintain currency; 400 citations are added per update.

The ACS extensively tested the database, and reports it to have been favorably evaluated by approximately 500 chemists and information scientists. According to the ACS the database will be "especially useful" to: information specialists; reference librarians and bibliographers, research chemists, bench chemists, biomedical and pharmaceutical researchers; and biomedical and pharmaceutical researchers; and environmentalists. The file is available from BRS with a royalty charge of $50 per connect hour. Offline prints have a royalty of $.28 per page.

INFORMATION SCIENCE ABSTRACTS *AVAILABLE*

DIALOG is now offering *Information Science Abstracts,* currently produced by the IFI/Plenum Data Company. The printed abstracting source was formerly published by Documentation Abstracts and sponsored by ASIS, the Special Libraries Association, and the American Chemical Society.

The database, available as File 202, includes 63,000 records from 1966 to the present; it is updated bimonthly with 1500 records. The file provides worldwide coverage of information science literature including government reports, proceedings, series, journal articles, patents and monographs. General subject fields covered are: information science and documentation; libraries and information services; information generation, reproduction and distribution; information recognition and description; storage and retrieval of information; utilization of information; and telecommunications. More than 450 journals are regularly scanned for inclusion in the database. The cost for searching *Information Sciences Abstracts* is $70 per connect hour and $.35 per full record printed offline.

Robotics Database Online

BRS is offering *Robotics,* a database produced by Cincinnati Milacron Industries. The file contains information on business and industrial applications of robotics, as well as technical innovations in the field. Sources of information include journals, newsletters, conference papers, reports, selected government publications, and books. Most citations include abstracts. Coverage is from 1980 to the present with selected retrospective coverage from 1970. The file contains primarily English language sources, with some foreign materials in order to "keep pace with international innovations in the industry."

Robotics contains approximately 4500 citations. It is updated monthly with 200 records. The royalty charge for searching this database is $30 per connect hour. Print costs are $.08 or $.11 for full records printed online; $.15 per citation for offline prints. Full-text photocopies of most articles and conference papers cited in the database are available from the producer.

PUBLICATIONS AND SEARCH AIDS

New POPLINE Tool Available

The *POPLINE Thesaurus Geographical Supplement* has been compiled by the POPLINE producers in cooperation with the United Nations-based Population Information Network (POPIN). It is an attempt to standardize the terms used to describe geographical regions and country names for indexing and retrieval of population literature. The supplement is based on terms used in the *Demographic Yearbook,* which is updated and published annually by the United Nations (UN) Statistical Office. The primary exception to the UN practice in this supplement is that geographic, rather then political, country names, are used to facilitate searching (e.g., CHINA rather than PEOPLE'S REPUBLIC OF CHINA).

The Geographical Supplement should be used in conjunction with the *POPLINE Thesaurus,* available from the Population Information Program or the Center for Population and Family Health Library/Information Program. It should simplify geographic searching in POPLINE. The basic purpose of this supplement is to increase thesaurus compatibility as well as compatibility among information systems and networks in the population field.

For a copy of the *Geographical Supplement* contact: Center for Population and Family Health Library/Information Program, Columbia University, 60 Haven Avenue, New York, NY 10032 or Population Information Program, The Johns Hopkins University, 624 North Broadway, Baltimore, MD 21205.

SCI-TECH IN REVIEW

Suzanne Fedunok, Editor

PUBLISHING OF SCIENTIFIC JOURNALS

Sanders, Howard J. Troubled times for scientific journals. *Chemical and Engineering News.* 61(22): 31-40; 1983 May 30.

This special report by a staff writer of *C & EN* magazine gives a factual and detailed account of the world of scientific journal publishing today, drawing on reports and studies done for learned societies like the AIP and ACS and on interviews with officers of those societies and publishers in the for-profit sector.

After explaining the reasons for rising costs of journals (composition costs, postage, paper, inflation), the article goes on to discuss the strategies publishers have used to increase their income (increased subscription prices, costs to advertisers and page charges; promotional advertising, increasing reprint fees), in an effort to offset what one publisher called "a vicious downward spiral."

The author reports that, while there is no hard evidence to support the contention, many publishers are convinced that extensive photocopying of articles is reducing significantly the number of subscriptions they sell. Other factors influencing the number of subscriptions seem to be document delivery systems and increased use of interlibrary loan systems by libraries. A representative of John Wiley and Sons is quoted as saying that publishers today are receiving on the average only 2% of the income to which they are entitled under the present copyright law.

Nevertheless, the number of journals keep growing. In ten years Pergamon Press increased the number of its scientific journals from 200 to 365, for example. The author's research leads to the conclusion that this is due to several factors: the increased specialization of science, the lag time in getting published in the established journals, and the need for scientists to "publish or perish."

The author's conclusion deals with the advent of the electronic journal and the pros and cons of outline publishing in science, as expressed by scientists and publishers.

A MODEL FOR REFERENCE SERVICE

Elchesen, Dennis Raymond. *Management of reference information services: a dynamic resource allocation model.* Livermore, CA: Lawrence Livermore National Laboratory; 1982 May. 434 pp. DE 82019879/UCRL-53261. PCA 19/MF A01.

In this PhD thesis, the author presents a dynamic resources allocation model and an associated computer program called collectively "REFSIM." The work was designed and tested at the library of the Lawrence Livermore Laboratory where three types of reference service were simulated: ready reference, in-depth reference, and current awareness services. The program considers the "inherently subjective" factors of human, information and equipment resources and components like requestor demand and degree of user satisfaction.

The model considers the fiscal side of reference service, providing a model for the generation and flow of monetary resources—charging and collection of service fees from requestors, allocation of funds, distribution of funds. The program also simulates the ability of the library to attract additional users through promotional activities.

The author concludes that his model is "a useful, although somewhat limited library management tool," the most valuable aspect of which is its predictive capability. It was designed to develop a quantitative tool that would enable a resource manager to determine the most cost-effective reference service configuration, to optimize the routine operations of the reference service, to predict changes, and to enable the manager to negotiate effectively with upper management.

There are 122 figures in the text, a bibliography of 258 items, and the computer simulation program is given in an appendix, with the caveat that, because of language restrictions, it cannot be readily transferred to other computing facilities.

INSTRUCTION IN CHEMICAL LITERATURE

Much of issue no. 12 of volume 59 of the *Journal of Chemical Education* is devoted to a "Symposium on Instruction in Chemical Literature". The following articles were of particular interest.

Gorin, George. An approach to teaching chemical information retrieval. *Journal of Chemical Education.* 59(12): 991-994; 1982 December.

The author, who is with Oklahoma State University, presented this paper at two meetings: to the 1979 ACS National Meeting and to the 1981 SLA Annual Conference. In it he gives an outline of a formal course of instruction, with many details including a list of the assignments and exercizes to be given.

Wiggins, Gary. The Indiana University Chemical Information Center program of chemical literature instruction. *Journal of Chemical Education.* 59(12): 994-997; 1982 December.
A brief history of the center, including a discussion of the courses taught there, is followed in an appendix by the bibliographies of two courses: Chemical documentation and Chemical information storage and retrieval methods and techniques.

Hendrickson, W. A. Library searching: an industrial users' viewpoint. *Journal of Chemical Education.* 59(12): 997-999; 1982 December.

The author makes the point that "it is imperative that the broadest, strongest background in library science be made available to students to help ensure their professional success." This will be especially true for the new industrial research chemist, who will be deprived of a graduate mentor and at the same time be required to practice a different kind of research methodology for the applied sciences.
The author believes that research in the industrial sector may be divided into three types, each of which builds on the other: the first stage of beginning with *Chemical Abstracts* and the usual reference sources available through the card catalog, a second step of citation

searching through sources like *Science Citation Index,* and the third stage of pursuing the topic through current awareness services and SDI programs.

Allen, Ferne C. Instruction in chemical literature: industrial librarian viewpoint. *Journal of Chemical Education.* 59(12): 999-1002; 1982 December.

The author gives a description of how the Technical Library at Texeco Chemical in Austen, Texas, conducts its course on the use of the library and the literature of chemistry. The article then gives suggestions on how librarians in academia could most thoroughly prepare students to use industrial libraries.

The strategy used at Texeco was to identify its user group, find out what was available for teaching chemical literature and modify it for their special audience, administer the program and follow up with a questionnaire. The author gives an outline of the course as it was taught and includes a list of the handouts and discussion topics as well as copies of the first questionnaire given to researchers as they entered the course and the second, follow-up questionnaire.

Academic librarians will find the list of eleven "General hints" a practical and useful one. The article concludes with a list and detailed suggestions about the kind of industrial information sources not usually covered in the standard academic courses.

ROBOTS IN LIBRARIES

Enter the robot librarian. *New Scientist.* 97(1347): 586; 1983 March 3.

This brief article describes the new "intelibot" system installed recently in the library of the Kanazawa Industrial University in Japan.

Small robots about the size of shoeboxes are guided by a central computer to page and load audio and video tapes for student users. The library has installed 60 booths equipped with video and audio cassette players and served by 34 robots, which were designed by Sony. This company feels that pictures carry more efficiently than print the increasing weight of information people have to assimilate, and it is using the 4500 students at the university as a test group for this idea.

For Product Safety Concerns and Information please contact our EU
representative GPSR@taylorandfrancis.com
Taylor & Francis Verlag GmbH, Kaufingerstraße 24, 80331 München, Germany

www.ingramcontent.com/pod-product-compliance
Lightning Source LLC
Chambersburg PA
CBHW052130300426
44116CB00010B/1839